Civility and Democracy in America
A Reasonable Understanding

Civility and Democracy in America

A Reasonable Understanding

Edited by
**Cornell W. Clayton
and Richard Elgar**

Washington State University Press
Pullman, Washington

Washington State University Press
PO Box 645910
Pullman, Washington 99164-5910
Phone: 800-354-7360
Fax: 509-335-8568
Email: wsupress@wsu.edu
Website: wsupress.wsu.edu

Printed and bound in the United States of America on pH neutral, acid-free paper. Reproduction or transmission of material contained in this publication in excess of that permitted by copyright law is prohibited without permission in writing from the publisher.

Library of Congress Cataloging-in-Publication Data

Civility and Democracy in America : A reasonable understanding / edited by Cornell W. Clayton and Richard Elgar.
    p. cm.
  Includes bibliographical references.
  ISBN 978-0-87422-312-5 (alk. paper)
1. Politics, Practical—United States—History. 2. Courtesy—Political aspects—United States—History. 3. Divided government—United States—History. 4. Democracy—United States. I. Clayton, Cornell W., 1960- II. Elgar, Richard, 1966-
  JK1726.R39 2012
  320.973—dc23

2012024273

Fine Quality Books from the Pacific Northwest

Table of Contents

Foley Institute Sponsorship   vii
Foreword   *Cornell W. Clayton and Richard Elgar*   ix

I. History

Introduction: Historical Perspectives on the Role of Civility   1
    in American Democracy
    Cornell W. Clayton

The Paradox of Civility   5
    Fredrik Logevall

What Isn't Nice? Civility and Social Movements   13
    Michael Kazin

Civil Rights, Civility, and Disruption   18
    Thomas J. Sugrue

II. Religion

Introduction: Faith in Religion, Civility, and Democracy   33
    Matthew Avery Sutton

Religion's Role in Contestations over American Civility   38
    Amanda Porterfield

Civility, Religion, and American Democracy: 48
    Some Cautionary Reflections
    Paul Boyer

Religious Pluralism and Civility   59
    Wade Clark Roof

III. Architecture

Introduction: Architecture and Civility   69
    Ayad Rahmani

Shared Difference: Citizenship and Civility in American   72
    Architecture and Urbanism
    Alan J. Plattus

Civility and Architectural Propriety   80
    Witold Rybczynski

On Democracy and Civility in American Architecture   86
    Joan Ockman

Public Buildings: Civility and Democracy   97
    Edward A. Feiner

IV. Philosophy and Ethics

Introduction: Philosophy and Ethics Themes   105
    Ann Levey

What Is Civility and How Does It Relate to Core   108
Democratic Values?
    Thomas Christiano

Reflections on Civility   119
    Joshua Cohen

The Circumstances of Civility   124
    Brian Leiter

V. Communication and Media

Introduction: Media and Civility in Context   131
    Lawrence Pintak

We Are Guests in Our Readers' Homes   135
    Peter Bhatia

Civility, Democracy, and the Mass Media   138
    Russell J. Dalton

News, Inclusion, and the Challenge of Civility   147
    Theodore L. Glasser

The Dangerous Amalgam of Modern Political Discourse   156
    Dietram A. Scheufele

Contributors   161

Foley Institute Sponsorship

In 2010 the National Endowment for the Humanities undertook an initiative to examine the role that civility plays in American democracy. As part of that initiative, the Thomas S. Foley Institute for Public Policy and Public Service at Washington State University, in collaboration with the Washington and Idaho humanities councils, organized a major conference, "Civility and Democracy in America," held in Spokane, Washington, in March 2011. Other conferences, also funded by the NEH, were hosted in March by the National Constitution Museum in Philadelphia, the American Bar Association in Chicago, and the California Council for the Humanities in Los Angeles, as part of a broader "National Dialogue on Civility and Democracy."

The three-day conference held in Spokane featured a distinguished group of scholars who discussed the complex and often counterintuitive relationships between civil behavior and democratic governance from several different humanities-based perspectives: history, philosophy, religion, art and architecture, and changing forms of media. In addition, the conference attracted many humanities practitioners, educators, students, and others from across the region. The essays in this book originated as presentations by the scholars at that conference. The views expressed are those of the individuals and do not necessarily reflect those of the National Endowment for the Humanities, the Thomas S. Foley Institute, or the Washington and Idaho humanities councils.

The Thomas S. Foley Institute for Public Policy and Public Service is a proud sponsor of this volume. The Foley Institute at Washington State University honors the service of Thomas S. Foley, former Speaker of the U.S. House of Representatives and U.S. Ambassador to Japan. The institute promotes public service, supports public policy research, and fosters education on public affairs. As part of its mission, it is pleased to be part of publishing this important volume.

Civility and American Democracy

Cornell W. Clayton and Richard Elgar

‖‖‖

T he role that civility plays in democratic government has long been a concern in the United States. From George Washington's 18th century *Rules of Civility & Decent Behaviour in Company and Conversation* ([1745] 1971), to *How to Behave: A Pocket Manual of Republican Etiquette* (Wells [1887] 2008), to more recent publications such as the Institute for Local Government's "Promoting Civility at Public Meetings" (2003), there have always been efforts to promote respectful behavior in public debates. In recent years, however, there is a sense that the level of civility in public life has reached a nadir. A study by Shandwick and Tate in 2011 found that 65 percent of Americans believe that the lack of civility in American public life is a major problem. Many reported experiencing a coarsening of manners during routine activities such as driving (72%) and shopping (65%), and even more (85%) believe that the level of political discourse has reached a new low (Shandwick and Tate 2011).

The perception that American democracy is in the midst of a civility crisis is not new. More than a decade ago major newspapers such as the *New York Times* (Johnson 1997) and *Washington Post* (Stinson 1998) began sounding the alarm about declining public manners and the divisive nature of public debate. The acrimonious tone of politics during the 1990s, both before and after the impeachment of President Clinton, also led to serious academic scrutiny about the role of civility in American democracy. From Eric Uslaner's *The Decline of Comity in Congress* (1993) and Stephen Carter's *Civility: Manners, Morals, and the Etiquette of Democracy* (1998), to Randall Kennedy's "The Case Against 'Civility'" (2001) and Virginia Sapiro's "Considering Political Civility Historically" (1999), academics began debating both the causes and consequences of declining civility in America's public discourse (see also Caldwell 1999).

A quick glance across today's political landscape and the cause of such concern becomes clear. From Tea Party protesters who shout down elected officials at town hall meetings, to Occupy Wall Street protesters who mock wealthier Americans, and political candidates who speak of "Second Amendment remedies" and activists who tote guns to political rallies, American politics is bitter, angry, and at times violent. President Obama's 2009 speech to a joint session of Congress was interrupted by Representative Joe Wilson (R-SC) shouting "You lie!" when Obama said his proposed health care plan would not cover illegal immigrants (CNN 2009). Similarly, President Bush was booed by some Democrats during his state of the union address in 2005 when he argued for privatizing social security. Given such recent episodes it is not surprising that the state of political discourse in the United States continues to be the subject of concern, both in popular media, such as the *New York Times* which recently lamented "So Much for Civility" (Collins 2009), and in a new wave of academic analyses such as Susan Herbst's *Rude Democracy* (2010).

The fear that incivility threatens the very fabric of American democracy peaked in the aftermath of the shooting of Arizona Representative Gabrielle Giffords (D) in January 2011. Following closely on the heels of a bitter midterm election, the shooting of Giffords and 18 innocent bystanders by a mentally-ill gunman shocked the nation and galvanized efforts to restore a more civil tone in American politics. At services honoring victims of the attack, President Obama called for a "new era of civility" (Cooper and Zeleny 2011). Soon thereafter a National Institute for Civil Discourse, with former presidents George H.W. Bush and Bill Clinton serving as honorary chairs, was established at the University of Arizona. The National Endowment for the Humanities also supported a series of conferences in spring 2011 examining the role of civility in democracy (of which the present volume is a product). Even presidential candidates such as Jon Huntsman pledged to run a different campaign—one that would not rely on negative advertising and would maintain a more respectful tone during the upcoming presidential election (Rutenberg 2011).

All such hopes, however, appeared to be dashed by the end of 2011. In August, the *Newsweek* cover pictured an irate-looking Representative Michelle Bachmann (R-MN) over the caption "Queen of Rage." Bachman, a presidential candidate, was at the time leading the Republican field in some polls because, the magazine suggested, she embodied the angry mood of the electorate. During the primary debates in 2011–2012 it became even clearer that hopes for a genteel campaign were over. Rick Perry, governor of Texas, accused Federal Reserve Chair Ben Bernenke of treason, intimating that he would be in personal danger in Texas. At another candidates' debate the audience broke into applause when Representative Ron Paul (R-TX) said that society should leave people to die if they do not have private health insurance and could not afford medical treatment (Kroll 2011). Jon Huntsman, who had kept his pledge to maintain a more civil tone in the campaign, attracted little support and made an early exit from the contest, leaving pundits to explain that he simply was not "angry enough" to connect with primary voters (Allen and Vandehei 2011, Gold 2011).

The uncivil nature of today's politics is often stoked by pervasive new forms of social media, political blogs, and partisan talk shows that routinely demonize those with whom they disagree. Political opponents are character-ized as "pinheads," "worst person in the world," or routinely compared to unsavory dictators such as Hitler or Stalin. There are also signs that the inci-vility of American public discourse is related to a deep paralysis in its elective institutions, which seem unable to address even the most pressing problems confronting the nation. During the summer of 2011, for example, partisan infighting turned a routine decision over raising the nation's debt ceiling into a protracted, name-calling contest that was followed by a downgrade of the nation's credit rating for the first time in history. Major political problems, ranging from a mounting national debt, to the growing polarization of wealth and economic opportunity and the need for fundamental reform of entitlement programs and the tax system, seem to be intractable problems mired in a partisan debate that lacks honesty, trust, and a willingness to compromise or find common ground.

The behavior of political leaders and the perceptions of those lead-ers among the public is important in a democracy. The ability to resolve problems in pursuit of a common interest ultimately rests on the ability of political leaders to "get along" and seek compromises that address common needs. Compromise obviously becomes more difficult in an environment where political leaders feel unfairly demonized and partisan followers are constantly told that their opponents pose an existential threat to the nation's most cherished values and institutions. Political leaders and their partisan followers do not necessarily need to agree, but the ability to consider differ-ent viewpoints and to respect one another as common citizens is a crucial aspect of democratic governance.

Is It New?

If American politics is suffering from a civility crisis today, it is not clear that this is much different from some other periods in history. In his essay in this volume, historian Fred Logevall writes: "The halcyon days of political geniality

"Mad Tom in a Rage"
*Devil: "Pull away, Pull away my son, don't fear, I'll give you all my assistance." Thomas
Jefferson: "Oh, I fear it is stronger rooted than I expected but with the assistance of my old
friend and a little more brandy, I'll bring it down."*
The Granger Collection, New York

and decorum in the United States never existed, not in the early days of the republic and not in the two-plus centuries that followed…(W)e would do well to remember that Americans have seldom trusted each other all that much, and have frequently questioned whether their Constitution embodies any principles they should uphold when the opposing party is in power."

Indeed, a survey of past periods reveals that politics has always been a rough and tumble business in the United States. Some previous periods of incivility were as bad as or worse than today. During the 1790s, for example, presidential campaigns were bitterly negative and a partisan press brutally attacked candidates on both sides. Conservative newspapers attacked John Adams as "a hideous hermaphroditical character, which has neither the force and firmness of a man, nor the gentleness and sensibility of a woman," while Federalist papers called Jefferson "a mean-spirited, low-lived fellow, the son of a half-breed Indian squaw, sired by a Virginia mulatto father." A common political cartoon of the period depicted a drunken Jefferson in the embrace of the devil as they together struggled to topple the pillars of republican government.

The political hatred was so intense before and after the election of 1800 that Adams and Jefferson, who had been close friends and trusted comrades during the Revolutionary War, ceased speaking to each other for nearly a quarter century. Nor was the animosity and bitterness of politics isolated. Two other major partisans of the time, Alexander Hamilton, a leader in the Federalist Party, and Aaron Burr, Jefferson's vice president, became so angry that they fought a duel in 1804, ruining Burr's political career and ending Hamilton's life.

During the elections of the 1820s, politics was again dominated by angry and bitter personal attacks. Supporters of John Quincy Adams often characterized Andrew Jackson as an ignorant ruffian. They accused him of murder, adultery, and called him "Andrew Jackass," which is how the donkey became the symbol of the Democratic Party. Jackson's supporters, on the other hand, spread rumors that Adams, while serving as ambassador to Russia, procured American girls for the sexual services of the Russian czar. The rumors were certainly untrue, but Jackson and his supporters nevertheless often referred to Adams as a "pimp" and a tyrant during the campaign (McNamara 2011).

In terms of sheer viciousness and violence, nothing compares to the politics before and during the Civil War. In 1856, Representative Preston Brooks of South Carolina viciously beat Senator Charles Sumner with a cane on the floor of the U.S. Senate. Sumner had delivered a speech against admitting new slave states into the union, and during the speech character-

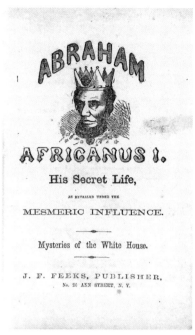

ized Illinois Senator Stephen Douglas as a "noise-some, squat, and nameless animal...not a proper model for an American senator," and accused South Carolina Senator Andrew Butler of having an "ugly mistress... that harlot, slavery" (U.S. Senate 2012). The election of 1860 was so fractious that Abraham Lincoln had to hire private security guards to help him sneak into Washington, D.C., at night out of the fear of an assassination attempt. Lincoln's election was soon followed, of course, by a complete breakdown in American democracy and a bloody civil war that engulfed the nation for the next four years. Yet, even while the nation was engaged in civil war, politics in the north remained bitterly divided and vicious. So-called Copperhead Democrats launched scurrilous attacks on Lincoln and Republicans. A typical pamphlet of the era, "Abraham Africanus," depicted Lincoln in pact with Satan to become a monarchical dictator (Del Mar 1864). Indeed, Copperhead rhetoric often invited violence against the president, such as a Wisconsin newspaper editor who wrote that "Lincoln is a fungus from the corrupt womb of bigotry and fanaticism...And if he is elected to misgovern for another four years, we trust some bold hand will pierce his heart with dagger point for the public good" (Summers 2009).

Throughout the 20th century there were more periods of deep division and incivility in American politics. For example, women suffragists were considered uncivil merely for expressing political views in public. They were derided in the press, spit upon in public, and arrested for engaging in peaceful political protests (Stevens 1995). Franklin Roosevelt's New Deal in the 1930s unleashed a paranoid and angry reaction that was often laced with anti-Semitic and racist undertones. It was during this time that Father Charles Coughlin pioneered the use of the radio talk show as a platform for political vitriol. His regular radio rants berated Roosevelt as "the great betrayer and liar," insinuating that the New Deal was part of a broader international Zionist conspiracy.

Some of the essays in this volume similarly recount the incivility and angry politics that accompanied the modern civil rights movement and the Vietnam War era in the United States. These periods of political turmoil witnessed not only organized pickets, protests, sit-ins, and flag-burning, but also violent responses in the form of police brutality, church- and cross-burnings, and political assassinations.

So it seems that American history is replete with periods of raucous politi-cal behavior and episodes of uncivil, even violent political behavior; such

Father Charles Coughlin
Public domain.

periods are not new, but are a part of the broader story of democracy in the United States. It is also true, however, that such periods are not the norm either. They are noteworthy precisely because they deviate from periods of "ordinary" political behavior, periods when the norms and conventions of civil conduct prevail and the passionate impulses of political debate are constrained.

What is Incivility and Why Now?

There is no widely agreed upon definition of civility or incivility as it applies to politics (Sapiro 1999). There are, however, similar themes that emerge in scholarly and academic discussions of it. Don Wolfensberger of the Woodrow Wilson Center, for example, argues that civility "is nothing more than the respectful way people interact with one another" (2011). P.M. Forni, direc-tor of the Civility Project at Johns Hopkins University, describes civility as a complex concept that "means being constantly aware of others and weaving restraint, respect, and consideration into the very fabric of this awareness" (2002). Yale Law Professor Stephen Carter defines civility as the "set of sacrifices we make for the sake of our common journey with others and out of…respect for the very idea that there are others" (1998). These concep-tions of civility indicate that civility applies to a sense of self and one's own behavior, but also an understanding and appreciation for others, especially when disagreements or differences of opinion arise.

Rather than a set of fixed manners or polite etiquette, political civility is better understood as a set of institutionalized practices or habits of thought that are both historically evolving and culturally relative. Thus, the norms that define civil political behavior in one context (say a formal meeting of a joint session of Congress) will be different than those in another context (say on a political blog or social media website). Even closely related institutional contexts may exhibit subtle but important differences in the norms and conventions that define appropriate behavior. For example, Joe Wilson's outburst during President Obama's speech to Congress in 2009 clearly transgressed codes of appropriate congressional behavior; however, heckling by an opposition politician during the prime minister's questions in the British House of Commons would raise few eyebrows.

While norms and conventions of civility can serve many purposes, a primary function of such institutions in democracy is to reinforce a commitment to the common bond of citizenship in the face of disagreement over policy. For example, the formal rules that require a respectful style of debate in Congress, or the customary congratulatory phone call that losing candidates are expected to make to election-day winners, or the ceremonial etiquette that accompanies major political events such as a presidential inauguration, are all practices that do not attempt to deny or suppress political disagreement as much as to channel them in a way that reminds partisans that beyond their policy divisions lies their commitment to common citizenship. To paraphrase an idea often repeated by President Obama (and borrowed from Lincoln and other presidents), these institutions and practices are intended to remind Americans that what unites them is greater than that which divides them.

Although isolated acts of political incivility may occur at any time, periods of prolonged incivility that threaten the very sense of common American citizenship have in the past accompanied periods of deep political cleavage. Periods such as the Jacksonian era in the 1820s, the Civil War, the New Deal in the 1930s, or the modern civil rights and Vietnam War era, were all periods when social and political developments so deeply divided Americans that questions arose about what it meant to be an "American" and who was included in the definition of citizenship. These were periods when the idea of citizenship was being contested and debated. Often these periods included major political or social movements that sought to extend the rights associated with citizenship to new groups (i.e. the movement for universal male suffrage in the 1820s, the abolitionist movement during the Civil War, the suffragists during the early 20th century, or the modern civil rights movement seeking greater equality for black Americans). They also included reactionary movements that opposed the expansion of citizenship (i.e. the Know Nothing movement in the mid-19th century, or the Ku Klux Klan of the mid-20th century). These periods are also often associated with what political scientists have termed "critical elections" or periods in which new political parties emerge or existing ones are reorganized to reflect the deep cleavages involved in redefining American citizenship (i.e. the emergence of Jefferson's Democratic-Republican Party in the 1790s, Jackson's Democratic Party in the 1820s, the Republican Party prior to the Civil War, or the New Deal Democratic Party in the 1930s). In other words, and not surprisingly, politics often becomes less civil and more passionate during the very times when politics matter most, when Americans are most divided and the terms of citizenship are contested.

If the United States has entered a new period of uncivil political behavior, we should therefore look first to the substantive issues dividing the country. From economic restructuring spurred by globalization, to growing income and wealth inequalities, protracted foreign wars in Iraq and Afghanistan, and rapid demographic changes, there are major political challenges confronting the United States and deep divisions over how they should be addressed. It is not surprising then that political passions may be running a little stronger and political fervor a little deeper. For all the concern about the style of politics, Americans may do well to remember that form usually follows substance. If Americans are behaving as if politics matter more today than during some previous periods, it is probably because it does.

Beyond the substance of political divisions, however, there may be other factors, more or less unique to this period in history, that also influences how Americans engage in politics. The evolution of religious practice in the United States in the past has served to both unify and divide the nation's diverse populations. The protestant perspective shared by the founders led to a historically-grounded view of civility, wherein religion helped to provide the basis upon which one's fellow citizens could expect to be treated. This shared religious outlook, together with a relatively homogenous group of newcomers to the United States, allowed for a commonly-understood foundation for norms and customs of political behavior and acted as what Wade Clark Roof's essay in this volume calls a "glue" that could undergird a common sense of citizenship that bound the nation. But over time, as Paul Boyer's essay points out, the increasing diversity of the population in the

United States and the concomitant wider range of religious beliefs led to deepening religious cleavages between those championing the traditional, predominantly protestant, worldview, and those that are more representative of a religious pluralism. Currently, diverse religious communities in the United States are often pitted against each other. Some fundamentalist religious movements dichotomize the world into good and bad, saved and sinner, even while many Americans celebrate a society that has become more tolerant, open, and diverse than ever before. Even more troubling, Boyer argues, is the increasing tendency of religious groups to ally themselves with one or another political party, creating the type of theologically based politics that prevents compromise and pragmatic discourse in politics.

But it is the media above all that demonstrates how a "hyperpolarized world," to borrow a phrase from Russell Dalton's essay in this volume, leads to increased invective and incivility. There is a certain democratic paradox in the proliferation of new, alternative media such as blogs and social networking sites and the way they have changed and shaped public discourse. On the one hand, the proliferation of new sources of political information and platforms for political news is profoundly democratic, allowing virtually anyone to communicate and disseminate their views and ideas. On the other hand, this fragmentation may make it more difficult to reach any understanding of the common good. Not only do new media allow the spread of misinformation and extremist views, it is also increasingly possible for individuals to tailor their media exposure to sources that reflect and confirm, rather than challenge, their existing perspectives and biases. This problem of media hyper-pluralism is exacerbated by the public's lack of media literacy and the inability to distinguish the quality and accuracy of different media sources (say the difference between *The New York Times* and a blog written by a private citizen). In his essay, Dietram Scheufele suggests that this process leaves us increasingly ill-prepared to interact in constructive ways with others with whom we disagree. As a result, we may feel more and more disenfranchised from the political system, not because of partisanship and incivility per se, but because of disengagement from the political process.

Moreover, the situation is no better in the mainstream political media world, which under economic pressures must increasingly focus on entertainment and ratings rather than on education and informing the public about complex policy matters. Oftentimes this leads to a style of "horse race" coverage of political campaigns and oversimplified storylines in which public issues are presented as dichotomies with little nuance or complexity. Ironically, while media organizations have changed the way they cover politics in order to attract ratings, Dalton notes that confidence in the media has reduced considerably over the past 40 years. It would appear therefore that Americans are convinced by the message, but less so (in this case) by the messenger.

Finally, the public square consists not only of the cyber world but also the physical world of buildings and public spaces. In America, there has been a panoply of architectural voices joining the "conversation" over time. But is this democratic equality of architecture a good thing? Witold Rybczynski argues that contemporary architecture has become increasingly uncivil. Rather than seeking harmonious relationships with their surroundings and a reverence for the community, recent architectural styles seek to be icono-clastic and discordant (think of the famed Guggenheim Museum in Bilbao or Sydney's award-winning opera house). Rybczynski suggests that this relatively new architectural incivility reflects social changes that have blurred distinctions between the public and private spheres, reflecting, perhaps, an expression of our contemporary world that has become less formal. Of course, as Joan Ockman notes in her essay, the consequences of incivility in architecture are usually not as high as in politics or religion, although, as she also points out, expressions of democracy tend to be most clearly realized in existing, actual spaces—most recently in Tahrir Square in Cairo, or in the Wisconsin State House of Representatives.

Civility and Its Relationship to Democracy

As the above discussion makes clear, the relationship between civility and democracy is more complicated than it may appear at first. Democratic decision-making requires vigorous contestation of ideas and interests, but also reasonable compromises born out of mutual trust, respect, and a com-mon sense of citizenship. Too much civility will stifle the former, while too little makes the latter impossible. During periods of deep political division in particular, insisting on the norms and customs of "civil" behavior, norms that simply encourage respectful debate in ordinary times, may be undemo-cratic in that they may serve to silence minority viewpoints. Indeed, some democratic critics of civility are skeptical of calls for greater civility, arguing that they are often efforts to suppress free expression and stifle perspectives that differ from those in power (Kennedy 2001, Herbst 2010).

The relationship between specific habits of civility and the actual per-formance of democracy is thus often dependent on the social relationships and patterns of power in a community. For example, many of the tactics employed by the modern civil rights movement were uncivil, in that they challenged accepted norms of "civilized behavior." Nevertheless, such tactics led to a more inclusive and more democratic American society. Conversely, when members of the Know Nothing Party in the 19th century, or members of the Ku Klux Klan in the 20th century, engaged in "uncivilized" acts that sought to exclude groups from full participation in American citizenship or to silence the views of groups seeking equal citizenship, their behavior seems profoundly undemocratic.

Similarly, over-emphasizing civility in the media may also act in an undemocratic way, by removing from the public sphere the full range of views, ideas, and disagreements. In short, while certain habits of thought and practices of civility may advance democratic debate in one context, they might be undemocratic in another. It is critical to recognize that history, community, and context matter a great deal in thinking about practices of civility and how they relate to democracy.

Seeking to account for the contextual quality of democratic civility, the philosopher Thomas Christiano argues in this volume that, more than a set of prescribed behaviors, it is a willingness to listen to others and refrain from silencing those with whom we disagree. Efforts to silence others can take many forms, including physical restraints such as imprisonment, intimidation, and threats of violence; shouting them down and drowning out their voices; or in less direct ways such as delegitimizing others' views by name-calling, insults, or ad hominem attacks. Joshua Cohen would go still further, suggesting that while civility does not require us to agree in policy disputes, or even to be polite in pressing our claims, it does require that policy arguments are made in terms that are open and accessible to all. It would be fundamentally uncivil to engage in policy debates using arguments that others in the community cannot reasonably be expected to accept as good arguments, such as one's private religious beliefs or moral conviction. Our common citizenship obligates us to use a common language or frame of argument for making policy claims. Thus, for example, one who argued that same same-sex marriage should be prohibited as a matter of policy on the grounds that it offends their private religious beliefs, would, in Cohen's account, be acting in a democratically uncivil way.

If the duty of civility demands self-restraint in the types of arguments we present during democratic debate, such a virtue may only work in practice if it is adopted by all parties. As Brian Leiter notes, in a dystopian setting, there is "no *obligation* of civility." In a political setting, where the goals and ends may be essentially contested, the *obligation* of civility simply may not exist, implying, perhaps, that both the nature and need for civility is situational and context-specific.

Conclusion

In his keynote address at the conference in Spokane, Stephen Carter argued that the central requirement of democracy is the willingness on the part of citizens to contest and potentially lose on issues that they care deeply and passionately about, while still remaining committed to the democratic enterprise. Carter's argument that democracy requires a commitment to our common citizenship, even in the face of deep disagreements over policy and programs, provides a useful way to think about the relationship between civility and democracy. In this view, the rules and practices of civility in democratic politics become similar to the rules and practices of sportsmanship in sports and games. Just as sportsmanship requires one to continue to play the game in good faith even while losing, civility in a democracy requires a commitment to the democratic endeavor and the common bonds of citizenship even when one loses policy debates that one cares deeply about.

How those common bonds of citizenship are understood is important in all democratic nations, but perhaps nowhere as much as the United States. Unlike many nations built around shared ethnic, religion, or cultural identities, the United States has no such natural bonds that hold it together. As Lincoln eloquently argued, it is a new kind of nation conceived in liberty and dedicated to a proposition that all are created equal. Past debates and fights over what that proposition stands for is the story of American democracy. The essays collected in this volume demonstrate the crucial yet sometimes paradoxical role that civility has played, and continues to play, in that story.

References

Allen, Mike, and Jim Vandehei. 2011. "The Problem with the Jon Huntsman Hype." *Politico*, June 26. politico.com/news/stories/0611/57753.html.

Caldwell, Mark. 1999. *A Short History of Rudeness: Manners, Morals, and Misbehavior in Modern America*. New York: Picador Books.

Carter, Stephen L. 1998. *Civility: Manners, Morals, and the Etiquette of Democracy*. New York: Basic Books.

CNN. 2009. "Joe Wilson Says Outburst to Obama Speech 'Spontaneous.'" CNNPolitics. com, September 10. cnn.com/2009/POLITICS/09/10/obama.heckled.speech.

Collins, Gail. 2009. "So Much for Civility." *The New York Times*, September 9. nytimes. com/2009/09/10/opinion/10collins.html.

Cooper, Helene, and Jeff Zeleny. 2011. "Obama Calls for New Era of Civility in U.S. Politics." *The New York Times*, January 12. nytimes.com/2011/01/13/us/13obama. html?pagewanted=all.

Del Mar, Alexander. 1864. *Abraham Africanus I: His secret life, as revealed under the mesmeric influence; Mysteries of the White House*. New York: J.F. Feeks.

Forni, P.M. 2002. *Choosing Civility: The Twenty-Five Rules of Considerate Conduct*. New York: St. Martin's Press.

Gold, Howard R. 2011. "Take a Deep Breath, GOP Voters." *The Independent Agenda*, December 14. independentagenda.com/politics-and-2012-election/take-a-deep-breath-gop-voters.

Herbst, Susan. 2010. *Rude Democracy: Civility and Incivility in American Politics*. Philadelphia: Temple University Press.

Institute for Local Government. 2003. "Promoting Civility at Public Meetings: Concepts and Practice." *Everyday Ethics for Local Officials*, October. ca-ilg.org/sites/ilgbackup.org/ files/resources/Everyday_Ethics_AugOct03.pdf.

Johnson, Dirk. 1997. "Civility in Politics: Going, Going, Gone." *The New York Times*, December 10. nytimes.com/1997/12/10/us/civility-in-politics-going-going-gone.html.

Kennedy, Randall. 2001. "State of the Debate: The Case Against 'Civility.'" *The American Prospect*, December 19. prospect.org/cs/articles?article=the_case_against_civility.

Kroll, Andy. 2011. "Debate: GOP Crowd Cheers Dying Uninsured Man, Ben Bernanke Treason Claim." *Mother Jones*, September 12. motherjones.com/mojo/2011/09/debate-crowd-cheer-dying-man-bernanke.

McNamara, Robert. 2011. "The Election of 1828 Was Marked By Dirty Tactics." About. com. history1800s.about.com/od/leaders/a/electionof1828.htm.

Rutenberg, Jim. 2011. "Huntsman Enters Race With Promise of Civility." *The New York Times*, June 21. nytimes.com/2011/06/22/us/politics/22huntsman.html?_r=2.

Sapiro, Virginia. 1999. "Considering Political Civility Historically: A Case Study of the United States." Presented at the annual meeting of the International Society for Political Psychology, Amsterdam, The Netherlands.

Shandwick, Weber, and Powell Tate. 2011. "Civility in America 2011." With KRC Research. webershandwick.com/resources/ws/flash/CivilityinAmerica2011.pdf.

Stevens, Doris. 1995. *Jailed for Freedom: American Women Win the Vote*. Edited by Carol O'Hare. Troutdale, OR: NewSage Press.

Stinson, Richard W. 1998. "Whatever Happened to Good Manners?" *The Washington Post*, July 24. LexisNexus Search Elite.

Summers, Mark Wahlgren. 2009. *A Dangerous Stir: Fear, Paranoia, and the Making of Reconstruction*. Chapel Hill: University of North Carolina Press.

Uslaner, Eric M. 1993. *The Decline of Comity in Congress*. Ann Arbor: Univ. of Michigan Press.

U.S. Senate. 2012. "The Caning of Senator Charles Sumner." senate.gov/artandhistory/ history/minute/The_Caning_of_Senator_Charles_Sumner.htm.

Washington, George. (1745) 1971. *Rules of Civility & Decent Behaviour in Company and Conversation: A Book of Etiquette*. Williamsburg, VA: Beaver Press.

Wells, Samuel R. (1887) 2008. *How to Behave: A Pocket Manual of Republican Etiquette*. Dodo Press.

Wolfensberger, Don. 2011. "Incivility Is Symptom of Larger Problem on Capitol Hill." *Woodrow Wilson International Center for Scholars*, July 7. wilsoncenter.org/publication/ incivility-symptom-larger-problem-capitol-hill.

I
History

Historical Perspectives on the Role of Civility in American Democracy

Cornell W. Clayton, Washington State University

||||||||||||||||||||||||||||||||||||||||||||||||||||||||||||||||||||||||||||||||||||||||||||||||||||||||||||||||||||||||||||||||||||||||||||||||

Many Americans believe that we are suffering from a long and steady decline in manners and the gradual coarsening of public discourse and behavior. According to this view, today's bitter partisan disputes and rude political behavior represent an unfortunate departure from past periods of civility and conviviality in our politics. However, the three historians contributing to this volume caution against such a romanticizing of the past. There never was a golden age of American political civility, and history is replete with periods that rival or surpass the bitterness and incivility of today's debates. From the nasty personal attacks that supporters of Adams and Jefferson hurled at each other during the divisive presidential campaign of 1800, to the duels and fights that occurred in our Congress in the run-up to the Civil War, to the scurrilous and anti-Semitic attacks lodged against Franklin Roosevelt and his administration by opponents in the 1930s, to the outright acts of violence that occurred on both sides of the modern civil rights movement, American politics has always been a rough and tumble business.

Yet if there have been periods of bitter, uncivil political behavior in the past, the cause of today's incivility and whether it is harmful to American democracy is less clear. In his essay "The Cacophonous Public Square," Fredrik Logevall argues that the "halcyon days of political geniality and decorum in the United States never existed, not in the early days of the republic and not in the two-plus centuries that followed." Indeed, Logevall argues that Americans have never trusted each other much, and have frequently questioned each other's motives and claims to common citizenship. Alexis de Tocqueville's classic study of American political culture in the 1830s depicted a nation of know-it-alls who were intellectually lazy and "frequently allow themselves to be borne away, far beyond the bounds of reason, by a sudden passion or a hasty opinion and sometimes gravely commit strange absurdities." But such a cacophonous public discourse was not a problem for democracy then nor should it necessarily be considered one today.

Logevall's essay calls our attention to the fact that democratic deliberation frequently depends on forthright, often contentious debate. Democratic discourse must be disruptive, skeptical, and question the claims made by its leaders. Too often the problem in American democracy, Logevall argues, is not "an absence of civility, but a surfeit of it." Lamenting the relative lack of tough debate that accompanied policy decisions during the early years of the Cold War, or during the build-up of American forces in Vietnam, or later during the prelude to the invasion of Iraq, Logevall argues that American democracy was ill-served by the civility of the times and the unwillingness of citizens and politicians alike to confront their leaders more forcefully. While it is fine to speak of a normative ideal in which civility involves respect for civic order and a toleration of differences, Logevall writes that we would also do well to remember Benjamin Franklin's famous admonition that the "first responsibility of every citizen is to question authority."

If incivility in itself is not a fundamental problem for democracy, the pervasive influence of new media may be. The intellectually lazy, know-it-all culture that has always been part of American politics is amplified by new forms of media that, Logevall writes, make it "easier to use misinformation to grease the wheels of incivility" by impoverishing the quality of public debate and dividing Americans in ways that make them less mindful of the common bonds of citizenship. While Americans have always engaged in raucous political debate, when we do disagree, Logevall quotes President Obama in urging us to adhere to "a tradition based on the simple idea that we have a stake in one another, and that what binds us together is greater than what drives us apart."

Michael Kazin's essay "What Isn't Nice? Civility and Social Movements" examines how civility and incivility are used as tactics by social movements. Kazin argues that context matters a great deal when evaluating whether specific acts of incivility are democratic or not. For example, the modern civil rights movement of the 1950s and 1960s turned the use of civil behavior on its head. Leaders of the movement used the tactic of peaceful protest purposely to provoke a violent response from whites in the South (in the case of Bull Connor against children) and to turn their opponents into moral villains. While today we honor Martin Luther King Jr. and his colleagues for advancing a more democratic America, Kazin argues that "it is debatable whether these civil rights heroes were practicing 'civility' in the contemporary understanding of that term."

Nevertheless, Kazin points out, when activists utilize tactics that Americans regard as "uncivil" it can also hurt their cause. As a strategic matter, popular disapproval of a group's tactics forces its supporters to be on the defensive and to defend their own actions instead of focusing public attention on the wrongs being protested. A well-known example of such a misstep was the burning of draft cards and American flags by anti-war demonstrators in the 1960s. Although the card and flag burners were only a small part of the anti-war movement, by defaming potent symbols of American patriotism, their actions bolstered support for the Nixon administration and alienated potential supporters of their cause.

One problem is that the line separating uncivil acts that are effective from ones that are ineffective and counterproductive is highly contingent on the context. Consider the difference between the air-traffic controllers (PATCO) strike of 1981, and the California farm workers' strikes against table-grape growers in the 1960s. Kazin points out that the former caused a backlash against the strikers, while the latter garnered nationwide sympathy and helped build an enduring movement to protect the rights of Mexican-Americans. There are other paradoxes raised if we consider how support for tactics or groups that are fundamentally uncivil and even horrific can nevertheless coexist with important democratic reforms. American Communists and their allies, Kazin argues, did much to promote important and lasting reforms in the area of civil rights, labor unionism, immigrant rights, and women's rights, all the while supporting a "monstrous" undemocratic regime in the Soviet Union.

These and other paradoxes demonstrate how difficult it is to distinguish in the abstract between civil and uncivil behavior and how either are related to democracy. Ultimately, we "should resist drawing lessons about the civility and incivility of movements to apply to all times and all kinds of movements." Context and history matter, Kazin argues, not only for what we regard as civil and uncivil behavior but for understanding what tactics will be successful and unsuccessful in advancing democratic causes.

Building on that theme, Thomas Sugrue's essay "Civil Rights, Civility, and Disruption" examines the multitactical nature of the modern civil rights movement. Like the previous two essays, his also urges us to de-mythologize the movement as one that was entirely civil and nonviolent. Indeed, "activists deployed a wide range of tactics that spanned a broad spectrum of civility and incivility." Some called for education and moral persuasion, while others took more adversarial positions, mounting lawsuits and fighting in the courts. Still others called for disruption, violence, and disorder, or at least used the threat of disorder to win concessions from those in power.

The success of the civil rights movement was due to its improvisational nature and the willingness of its leaders to adopt different tactics at different times. Although moral persuasion and dialogue was a dominant theme in the movement, and was often successful at building public sympathy for it aims, dialogue alone was not enough to produce political and social change. Activists had to use tactics that would by most accounts be called uncivil and even coercive. Those tactics ranged from lawsuits to protests, boycotts, strikes, and civil disobedience. Whether in Birmingham in 1963 or Newark in 1967, the struggle for racial equality progressed, Sugrue argues, only when activists mixed their tactics—"when they combined the civil and the disruptive, when they worked to change hearts and minds but also to transform institutions, often by any means necessary." Indeed, looking back at the 1960s through a prism of contemporary debates about civility overlooks the fact that to those whose social positions were threatened by civil rights reforms, the whole struggle was uncivil. Sugrue reminds us that J. Edgar Hoover denounced Martin Luther King Jr. as the "most dangerous Negro in America." Civil rights protestors were characterized by southern authorities as "outside agitators," and groups such as CORE, the SCLC, and the Black Panthers were often derided as "un-American." Civility and incivility, it seems, is in the eye of the beholder. To those who wish to maintain the status quo, any challenge to existing order, whether by picketers, protestors, or preachers is likely to be regarded as uncivil as much because of the message as the methods.

The philosopher Georg Wilhelm Friedrich Hegel observed that the only sure lesson of history is that nations fail to learn from it.[1] If Hegel is correct, then perhaps it is not surprising that recent acts of rude and confrontational political behavior have been met with laments about a general decline in civility and dire warnings about its implications for democracy. On the other hand, if the collective lesson from these three essays is that situation and motive matters, then these essays force us to at least consider such acts more fully in the context of contemporary American society and the political issues that divide us.

Note

1. "What experience and history teach is this—that nations and governments have never learned anything from history, or acted upon any lessons they might have drawn from it." Georg Wilhelm Friedrich Hegel, *Lectures on the Philosophy of History* (1832), Introduction.

The Paradox of Civility

Fredrik Logevall, Cornell University

|||||||||||||||||||||||||||||||||||||||||||||||||||||||||||||||||||||||||||||||||||||||||||||||||||||||||||||||||||||||||||||||||||

W e should resist golden-ageism on the subject of civility and American democracy. The halcyon days of political geniality and decorum in the United States never existed, not in the early days of the republic and not in the two-plus centuries that followed. True, the belligerence and petulance were more intense in some periods than others, the verbal fisticuffs more bruising. And true, it seems we're in a notably cantankerous era today. But we would do well to remember that Americans have seldom trusted each other all that much, and have frequently questioned whether their Constitution embodies any principles they should uphold when the opposing party is in power.

Thus in the much-exalted founding generation, we find John Adams describing Thomas Paine as the "mongrel" offspring of "a wild boar and a bitch wolf" (Taylor 2010, xx), and Paine wondering whether George Washington was "an apostate or an imposter; whether [he had] abandoned good principles, or whether [he] ever had any" (Ayer 1988, 162). Alexander Hamilton, meanwhile, said of Thomas Jefferson: "He is not scrupulous about the means of success, nor very mindful of truth and…he is a contemptible hypocrite" (Chernow 2004, 634). To which Jefferson answered: "I will not suffer my retirement to be clouded by the slanders of a man whose history, from the moment at which history can stoop to notice him, is a tissue of machinations against liberty of the country which has not only received and given him bread, but heaped its honors on his head" (Wood 2009, 157).

Later, during the 1864 presidential campaign, Northern Union Democrats distributed incendiary pamphlets against Abraham Lincoln, including one labeled "Abraham Africanus" and another claiming that a vote for Lincoln was a vote for racial mixing (McPherson 2003, 695). Closer to our own day anti-New Dealers castigated President Franklin D. Roosevelt in incendiary terms, some of them hinting that he was a mere puppet of international Jewish bankers. In 1951, Senator Joseph McCarthy unleashed an invective against Secretary of Defense George C. Marshall, a former Army chief of staff and secretary of state, accusing Marshall of willfully betraying American interests over several years. There was a "baffling pattern" to Marshall's decisions, McCarthy charged, which somehow always redounded to the benefit of the Kremlin. The steep decline in America's relative strength since the end of World War II didn't "just happen"; it was "brought about, step by step, by will and intention," the consequence not of mistakes but of a treasonous conspiracy, "a conspiracy on a scale so immense as to dwarf any previous such venture in the history of man" (Hofstadter 1964).

Or consider Lyndon B. Johnson's oft-quoted characterization of House Minority Leader Gerald R. Ford, made after Ford questioned the Johnson administration's handling of the Vietnam War: "He's a nice fellow but he spent too much time playing football without a helmet" (Davis 2011, 505).

How to explain this tradition of mistrust and coarseness in the nation's political discourse? And how concerned should we be by its persistence into the 21st century? For answers we could do worse than turn to Alexis de Tocqueville's two-volume masterpiece, *Democracy in America* (1835-1840 [1966]), arguably still the most incisive inquiry into the society, polity, and culture of the United States ever published. Much has changed in this country in the 170-plus years since the Frenchman wrote, but to reread the work now is to be struck by how much of his analysis endures—and how much of it defies easy categorization.

In the United States, Tocqueville writes in volume two, "When all men see each other at close quarters, have together learned the same things and led the same life, there is no natural inclination for them to accept one of their as a guide and follow him blindly; one hardly ever takes on trust the opinion of an equal of like standing with oneself.... As men grow more like each other, the dogma concerning intellectual equality gradually creeps into their beliefs, and it becomes harder for any innovator whosoever to gain and maintain great influence over the minds of a nation" (616).

In other words, expertise is suspect and to be doubted at all times. Such is the power of the belief in equality. "When it comes to the influence of one man's mind over another," the Frenchman bitingly wrote, "that is necessarily very restricted in a country where the citizens have all become more or less similar, see each other at very close quarters, and since they do not recognize any signs of incontestable greatness or superiority in any of their fellows, are continually brought back to their own judgment as the most apparent and accessible test of truth. So it is not only confidence in any particular man which is destroyed. There is a general distaste for accepting any man's proof of anything. So each man is narrowly shut up in himself, and from that basis makes the pretension to judge the world" (394).

If this was Tocqueville's depiction of American political culture in the 1830s, it retains its resonance today, some 170 years later. The United States is a nation of know-it-alls, and it makes for a cacophonous political arena. It was always thus. South Carolina Representative Joe Wilson's "You lie!" outburst during Barack Obama's address to a joint session of Congress in September 2009 might seem unprecedented, but the eruption would not have shocked Tocqueville. Americans, after all, often allow themselves to be "carried away, far beyond the bounds of common sense, by some sudden passion or hasty opinion. They will in all seriousness do strangely absurd things" (586).

Nor, it should be emphasized, was Tocqueville unduly troubled by this inherent messiness in the American public square. For one thing, he was coming from France, where his family had experienced first-hand and for generations the denial of individual liberty and the centralization of political and administrative power. His parents suffered imprisonment for political reasons and barely escaped execution, winning their release only after the ultra-radical Terror phase of the French Revolution waned. Hence the appeal to the young Tocqueville of America's decentralized system, and of the relative weakness of executive power from the presidency to the governorships. Moreover, Tocqueville emphasized, it was only through this often unruly process of democratic contestation and compromise that Americans came to achieve the common good, through what he called "the doctrine of self-interest properly understood." That is to say, Americans discerned that concern for the interests of others could, in the long run, also serve one's own interests; he called it "enlightened selfishness" (500). By adhering to this principle, American democracy appeared to be striking the proper balance between public and private interests in a way that the French, with their fatal unwillingness to reach accommodations with each other, had failed to do.

Tocqueville knew perfectly well that women, most African Americans, and most Native Americans did not have the right to vote. Nevertheless, next to highly restrictive property requirements for voting in Europe, the United States seemed to him to be functioning on the basis of popular sovereignty. And much more than was the case in his own country, Americans from different backgrounds managed to find common ground, or at least to tolerate their differences. This was the essence of the democratic system: the willingness to accept compromise solutions instead of demanding complete victory over one's opponents. In historian James Kloppenberg's (2010) words, it means "squabbling about differences, reaching tentative agreements, then immediately resuming debate" (178).

Yet there's a paradox here. For the know-it-allism can also make people intellectually lazy and content to follow the pack on any given topic. "I know no country in which, speaking generally, there is less independence of mind and true freedom of discussion than in America," Tocqueville wrote (235). A debatable assertion, surely, even in the context of the time the Frenchman wrote, yet he was on to something. A healthy political discourse depends on honest and forthright contention. Real civility can be disruptive, can question the claims and motives of leaders, can be skeptical. A healthy and robust democracy depends on such questioning and risks grievous damage without it.

I think about this with respect to my own field of specialization, post-1945 foreign relations history. Here one could argue that the problem too often has not been an absence of civility, but a surfeit of it. In the early Cold War, for example, the range of acceptable opinion in Washington vis-à-vis policy toward the Soviet Union narrowed so dramatically that it effectively ceased to exist, as Democrats and moderate Republicans, afraid of being tagged with the "soft on communism" label, avoided asking hard questions about the Truman administration's expansive policy of containment, about the nature of the Soviet threat, and about how to distinguish between Stalin's hostility and his intentions and his capabilities. Savvy candidates for national political office knew that vociferous anticommunism should be their default posture on the campaign trail; as a result, beginning in the late 1940s, the range of acceptable political opinion narrowed dramatically. Any possibility for serious debate on policy options vis-à-vis the communist world more or less disappeared, as those on the left and center-left who might have offered a different vision lost political as well as cultural sanction.

As author David Halberstam (2002) would write of the early Cold War period: "Rather than combating the irrationality of the charges of softness on communism and subversion, the Truman Administration, sure that it was the lesser of two evils, moved to expropriate the issue, as in a more subtle way it was already doing in foreign affairs. So the issue was legitimized; rather than being the property of the far right, which the centrist Republicans tolerated for obvious political benefits, it had even been picked up by the incumbent Democratic party" (108-09).

Or consider the Vietnam War. Lyndon Johnson's massive escalation of U.S. involvement in Vietnam in 1964-65 occurred, I have argued elsewhere, within a "permissive context" (Logevall 1999, 400-04). The near-unanimous passage in August 1964 of the Gulf of Tonkin Resolution—which gave Johnson wide latitude to wage war in Southeast Asia as he saw fit—should not obscure the fact that the most respected, most senior Democratic legislators on Capitol Hill privately opposed large-scale increase in the American commitment. Nor were they alone. Exact numbers are hard to come by, but certainly in the Senate a clear majority of Democrats—including the senior leadership on foreign policy—and moderate Republicans were either downright opposed to Americanization or ambivalent; meanwhile, vocal proponents of taking the war to North Vietnam were strikingly few in number. Publicly, though, the vast majority of lawmakers voiced staunch support for standing firm in the war, not merely in August 1964 but in the critical months that followed. In the press, too, leading newspapers were disinclined to ask tough questions in the months of decision, to probe deeply into administration claims regarding the situation on the ground in South Vietnam and the need to take new military measures. Among the broader public, meanwhile, apathy was the order of the day. Most Americans were too preoccupied with their daily lives to give much thought to a small Asian country thousands of miles away.

The Iraq invasion of 2003 likewise occurred within a permissive context. It was the 1965 (non)debate redux. In the lead-up to the invasion reporters for leading newspapers—including the *New York Times* and the *Washington Post*—accepted with little question administration claims regarding the intentions and capabilities of Iraqi leader Saddam Hussein. By and large, they failed to probe beneath the surface, failed to give serious attention to the views of skeptics. The same was true of editorial writers and columnists across the country, and of television pundits and talk-show hosts. On Capitol Hill, meanwhile, most lawmakers of both parties were content to avoid asking too many questions—or, if they did ask them, to quickly add that they too wanted to be "tough on Saddam." It's difficult to avoid the conclusion that there was a certain willingness to be deceived among lawmakers, a willingness to be strong-armed by the White House. Many were quite content to escape responsibility from a murky policy issue for which few of them had a clear prescription.

Lincoln Chafee of Rhode Island, the only Republican senator to vote against giving Bush authorization to remove Saddam Hussein by force, in his memoirs chastises senior Democrats for their lack of courage in the debate. "The top Democrats were at their weakest when trying to show how tough they were," he writes. "They were afraid that Republicans would label them soft in the post-September 11 world, and when they acted in political self-interest, they helped the president send thousands of Americans and uncounted innocent Iraqis to their doom" (Chafee 2008, 93).

The permissive context extended also to the general public. Though there were antiwar demonstrations in small and large cities across the country in late 2002 and early 2003, and though numerous bloggers questioned what they saw as the rush to war, most Americans in these months were content to go along with the alarmist White House claims concerning the threat posed by Hussein's regime. Few had a deep knowledge of the issues at stake or an inclination to educate themselves, and as such were inclined to follow the government's lead. Polling data showed little popular enthusiasm for attacking Iraq, but broad trust in Bush's leadership. Whereas right after 9/11 a mere 6 percent believed that Al Qaeda leader Osama bin Laden had collaborated with Saddam Hussein, by the eve of the invasion the figure had risen to 66 percent. A majority now even believed that Iraqis had been among the September 11 hijackers (Zeller 2003). Few legislators reported widespread demands from their constituents to hold more hearings or pressure the administration for more proof that preventive war was needed. University campuses by and large were quiescent places in the weeks prior to the invasion.

Lack of civility wasn't a problem in these cases; quite the contrary. The searching questioning that democracy demands—not least when the issue concerns wars of choice and whether to enter them, as was the case with Vietnam and Iraq—was seldom seen. All of which suggests that while it is proper to speak of a normative ideal, in which civility involves respect for civic order, toleration of differences, and conduct worthy of a citizen, we should also be ever mindful of Benjamin Franklin's famous admonition: "The first responsibility of every citizen is to question authority." The nation's contemporary history shows the continuing resonance of Franklin's dictum, though perhaps also the need to amend it slightly, even at the risk of lessening its rhetorical power: "The first responsibility of every citizen is to become informed on the issues, and to question authority."

What, then, of today? Has the American public square ceased to function in the way Tocqueville and so many other observers after him described? History suggests skepticism is in order. More likely, our pervasive media presence is just making more evident and pronounced the uncivil tendencies that have always been in the culture. Whereas in Tocqueville's time (and for more than a century thereafter) it was possible to ignore vitriolic partisan attacks by simply neglecting the newspaper or steering clear of the neighborhood tavern, that's no longer an option. The amplification mechanisms are just too strong, too varied.

Therein lurks a danger, of course, namely that the new media can make it easier to use misinformation to grease the wheels of incivility. In August 2009, as rumors swirled that Barack Obama's health care plan would create "death panels," the president told an audience in New Hampshire: "That's what America is about, that we have a vigorous debate. That's why we have a democracy. But I do hope that we will talk with each other and not over each other, because one of the objectives of democracy and debate is that we start refining our own views because maybe other people have different perspectives, things we didn't think of. Where we do disagree, let's disagree over things that are real, not these wild misrepresentations that bear no resemblance to anything that's actually been proposed."

Perhaps it says something about our current age that Obama has made such frequent references to civility and the need to maintain it, to overcome what he calls the "industry of insult." A line from his 2006 book, *The Audacity of Hope*, sticks in the mind: Americans, he writes, should adhere to the "tradition that stretched from the days of the country's founding to the glory of the civil rights movement, a tradition based on the simple idea that we have a stake in one another, and that what binds us together is greater than what drives us apart" (4).

References

Ayer, A.J. 1988. *Thomas Paine*. Chicago: University of Chicago Press.

Chafee, Lincoln. 2008. *Against the Tide: How a Compliant Congress Empowered a Reckless President*. New York: Thomas Dunne.

Chernow, Ron. 2004. *Alexander Hamilton*. New York: Penguin.

Davis, Kenneth C. 2011. *Don't Know Much About History: Everything You Need to Know About American History*. New York: HarperCollins.

Halberstam, David. 2002. *The Best and the Brightest*. 20th anniversary ed. New York: Random House.

Hofstadter, Richard. 1964. "The Paranoid Style in American Politics." *Harper's*, November.

Kloppenberg, James T. 2010. *Reading Obama: Dreams, Hope, and the American Political Tradition*. Princeton, NJ: Princeton University Press.

Logevall, Fredrik. 1999. *Choosing War: The Lost Chance for Peace and the Escalation of War in Vietnam*. Berkeley: University of California Press.

_____. 2010. "Anatomy of an Unnecessary War: The Iraq Invasion." In *The Presidency of George W. Bush: A First Historical Assessment*, edited by Julian E. Zelizer. Princeton, NJ: Princeton University Press.

McPherson, James M. 2003. *The Illustrated Battle Cry of Freedom: The Civil War Era*. New York: Oxford University Press.

Obama, Barack. 2006. *The Audacity of Hope: Thoughts on Reclaiming the American Dream*. New York: Crown.

Taylor, Alan. 2010. "Introduction," *Thomas Paine's Common Sense*. Cambridge, MA: Belknap Press of Harvard University Press.

Tocqueville, Alexis de. (1835-1840) 1966. *Democracy in America*. Edited by J.P. Mayer and Max Lerner. Translated by George Lawrence. New York: Harper & Row.

Wood, Gordon S. 2009. *Empire of Liberty: A History of the Early Republic, 1789-1815*. New York: Oxford University Press.

Zeller, Tom. 2003. "How Americans Link Iraq and Sept. 11." *New York Times*, March 2. nytimes.com/2003/03/02/weekinreview/the-nation-how-americans-link-iraq-and-sept-11.html.

What Isn't Nice?
Civility and Social Movements

Michael Kazin, Georgetown University

|||||||||||||||||||||||||||||||||||||||||||||||||||||||||||||||||||||||||||||||||||||||||||||||||||||||||||||||||||||||||||||||||||

C onsider the lyrics of a song by Malvina Reynolds, written in 1964 about the tactics being used by the civil rights movement:

> *It isn't nice to block the doorway,*
> *It isn't nice to go to jail,*
> *There are nicer ways to do it,*
> *But the nice ways always fail.*
> *It isn't nice, it isn't nice,*
> *You told us once, you told us twice,*
> *But if that is Freedom's price,*
> *We don't mind.*
>
> *It isn't nice to carry banners*
> *Or to sit in on the floor,*
> *Or to shout our cry of Freedom*
> *At the hotel and the store.*
> *It isn't nice, it isn't nice,*
> *You told us once, you told us twice,*
> *But if that is Freedom's price,*
> *We don't mind.* (Reynolds 1964)

This text raises a number of interesting questions about the uses, limits, and meaning of civility—both language and behavior—in the history of social movements, particular American ones.

First, contrary to Reynolds' lyrics, the behavior of the civil rights movement from the 1950s to the mid-1960s was not "uncivil," at least in the contemporary meaning of that term. When activists engaged in peaceful disobedience, they did refuse to recognize their white racist adversaries as rational opponents. For that matter, they sometimes denounced white liberals for compromising with the movement's sworn enemies—as during the Mississippi Freedom Democratic Party's challenge at the Democratic national convention in 1964.

But one should really turn the "it isn't nice" line around. As the late historian Kenneth Cmiel observed, the nonviolent protests in the South and parts of the North inverted the social order by acting civilly, if at times illegally, which led local whites to act violently in response. Often, the tactics of movement organizers were explicitly intended to provoke just such a reaction (1994).

A famous example occurred in the spring of 1963 during the campaign led by the Southern Christian Leadership Conference (SCLC) in Birmingham, Alabama. At first, the demonstrators (most of whom were black adults) who marched into downtown were tolerated by city police, under the command of Eugene "Bull" Connor. A state court then enjoined the SCLC from organizing further protest marches. Martin Luther King Jr. defied the ruling and went to jail on Good Friday. There he wrote the now iconic "Letter from Birmingham Jail," in response to local white clergymen who called the demonstrations "unwise and untimely" (1963). King was released on Easter Sunday, frustrated that the resurrection of his movement was not occurring. He told Wyatt Walker, the key local strategist for the SCLC, "Wyatt, you've got to find some way to make Bull Connor tip his hand" (Isserman and Kazin 2008).

The way they found was to mobilize local schoolchildren. On May 2, a thousand children filed out of the 16th Street Baptist Church and overwhelmed Connor's men. The next day, when the children's march took off again, city firemen turned on high-pressure hoses to drive them off. German shepherds from the police K-9 squads tore into their flesh. That night, TV viewers all across the nation saw white Southern authorities at their worst. The angry response to the images made it inevitable that President John F. Kennedy would propose a major civil rights bill—and probable that it would pass.

So was it "civil" to organize nonviolent protests in order to provoke a violent response—against children? Or to make Bull Connor and those who supported him, such as Governor George Wallace, into moral villains? "It is impossible to censure measures without condemning men," declared William Plumer, a senator from New Hampshire in the 1790s (Wood 2009, 160). Today, everyone from left-wing activists to mainstream Democrats to conservatives like Glenn Beck honors King and his colleagues. But it's debatable whether these civil rights heroes were practicing "civility" in the contemporary understanding of that term.

At the same time, when most Americans do regard a particular movement's behavior as uncivil, their opinion inevitably hampers the fortunes of that movement. Their disapproval forces activists and their supporters to defend their actions instead of keeping the public's attention on the wrongs they are protesting. Well-known examples of such false steps in the 1960s include the burning of draft cards and American flags by some anti-war demonstrators and the Black Panther Party's ubiquitous slogan, "Off the Pigs"—which meant, of course, "kill the police." The draft card and flag burners were a tiny part of the anti-war movement, and they were neither engaging in nor even advocating violence. But because they were defaming potent symbols of American patriotism, their actions bolstered support for the Nixon administration's war policy. The political theorist Michael Walzer has written about the need for left-wing intellectuals and activists to practice "connected criticism"—to show respect for the sensibilities of one's community and one's nation. Believing they were attacking evil authorities, some radicals in the 1960s unintentionally mobilized mass anger against their own uncivil behavior (1988).

But the line that separates nonviolent acts that are uncivil but effective from ones that are ineffective and counterproductive can shift over time. For example, in the 1930s, sit-down strikes in auto factories and other manufacturing plants and some department stores helped win union recognition for millions of wage-earners. But attempts to use similarly coercive tactics in the 1946 strike wave helped turn public sentiment against organized labor.

For that matter, strikes themselves, even when quite legal and scrupulously nonviolent, have often been perceived as uncivil when the workers involved are viewed as either privileged or essential to the operation of a key industry. Think of the difference between the air-traffic controllers (PATCO) strike of 1981 or almost any strike today by school teachers—both groups of public employees vital to everyday life—and that of California farmworkers' strikes against table-grape growers in the 1960s. The former caused a backlash against the strikers, while the latter garnered nationwide sympathy and helped build an enduring Mexican-American movement.

In her song, Malvina Reynolds was clearly aware of the shifting line between civil and uncivil. Her lyric implies that those who use uncivil behavior do so only when they are fairly certain it will be effective: "if" that's freedom's price, we don't mind. She did not take for granted that there was a moral justification for breaking the law—even when the laws in question were bolstering a manifestly unjust racist system.

But perhaps we should have a broader definition of incivility, one that allows us to evaluate the morality of an activist's overall worldview. Perhaps the political ideology of the woman who wrote "It Isn't Nice" is also relevant to the question of civility. In the 1940s and 1950s, Reynolds was active in the Popular Front in Northern California, and was a registered Communist voter in that state, where she married a Communist Party member and organizer. Later, in an interview, she recalled that "The [Communist] movement was our community." Reynolds left the party at an undetermined date because its leaders "had no concept of what I was doing," not because she disagreed with Communist politics (Lieberman 1989, 77-78). Her song, which praised peaceful, if uncivil behavior, was sung by people who helped win equal rights for Americans of color and, more generally, helped make the United States a more tolerant and diverse society.

Yet the movement to which Reynolds belonged was in thrall to and took direction from one of the most brutal, violent, and destructive regimes in all of history. In the United States, the Communists and their allies accomplished much of lasting value in the spheres of civil rights, labor unionism, immigrant rights, and women's rights. But its fatal flaw was to believe that the monstrous regime in the Soviet Union was the harbinger of a more humane and democratic world (Kazin 2011). So what does that paradox mean for a history of civility? If nothing else, it shows how difficult it is, in the history of social insurgencies and in politics more generally, to draw a line between civil beliefs and behavior and their opposites.

In the end, I think we should resist drawing lessons about the civility and incivility of movements to apply to all times and all kinds of movements. Sometimes, it is certainly essential to lay down strict moral lines—to recognize what is not just unfair but evil and to use precise but passionate language to make that clear. But in every case, it's better to do so in a way that allows you to reach the unconvinced and/or inactive instead of in ways that force them on the defensive, believing they have no alternative but to oppose everything you stand for and want to accomplish.

A recent example of a movement that protested intelligently and successfully was the insurgency that helped topple the Mubarak regime in Egypt in the winter of 2011. The resisters in- and outside Cairo's Tahrir Square turned back the repression of the regime by stating eloquently and clearly both their grievances and their demands—and refused to give in until they won. But they never initiated violence or defamed institutions—the army and the mosque—that nearly all Egyptians cherished. And they were inclusive of all sections of the population without diluting the power of their message. They embodied the highest sort of civility—respectful, democratic, peaceful, and strategically effective. By themselves, their actions did not and could not transform Egypt into the just and tolerant society they desired. But they did make it possible for millions of Egyptians to imagine such a society was possible. In other words, they took the first, most necessary step toward realizing their ultimate goal.

References

Cmiel, Kenneth. 1994. "The Politics of Civility." In *The Sixties: From Memory to History*, edited by David Farber, 267. Chapel Hill: University of North Carolina Press.

Isserman, Maurice, and Michael Kazin. 2008. *America Divided: The Civil War of the 1960s*, 3rd ed. New York: Oxford University Press, 89-92.

Kazin, Michael. 2011. *American Dreamers: How the Left Changed a Nation*. New York: Knopf, chapter five.

King, Martin Luther, Jr. 1963. "Letter from Birmingham Jail." April 16. mlk-kpp01.stanford. edu/index.php/encyclopedia/documentsentry/annotated_letter_from_birmingham.

Lieberman, Robbie. 1989. *"My Song Is My Weapon": People's Songs, American Communism, and the Politics of Culture, 1930-50*. Urbana: University of Illinois Press, 15.

Reynolds, Malvina. 1964. "It Isn't Nice." Song lyrics and music. Schroder Music Company. people.wku.edu/charles.smith/MALVINA/mr073.htm.

Walzer, Michael. 1988. *The Company of Critics: Social Criticism and Political Commitment in the Twentieth Century*. New York: Basic Books.

Wood, Gordon. 2009. *Empire of Liberty: A History of the Early Republic, 1789-1815*. Oxford: Oxford University Press, 160.

Civil Rights, Civility, and Disruption

Thomas J. Sugrue, University of Pennsylvania

F ew images from the civil rights struggle are more indelible than the famous photo of a Trailways Bus, engulfed in flame, on the side of the road in Anniston, Alabama, in April 1961. Nonviolent protestors aboard the bus, black and white, had deliberately breached southern Jim Crow laws. For that transgression, they were subject to vicious attacks. As they disembarked the burning bus, angry whites pummeled them. The Freedom Riders, organized by the Congress of Racial Equality (CORE), were aboard the bus that April day in hopes of creating a "beloved community" of black and white, equal in the eyes of God and under the law. To that end, they sat together, violating southern state laws that required black passengers to give up their seats to white passengers and retreat to the back of the bus. At station stops, they breached the rules of American apartheid. For them the colored and white only drinking fountains and bathrooms were a disgrace; the racially separate waiting rooms were humiliating. The Freedom Riders were peaceful and soft spoken, even as they openly flouted what they considered to be unjust laws.

In the face of violence, the Freedom Riders faced accusations that their actions were uncivil. Southern law enforcement authorities, eager to delegitimize the movement, arrested them and charged them with disturbing the peace. White civic leaders stigmatized them as communists and disparaged them for stirring up discontent where none existed. They were "outside agitators" who intentionally intended to provoke conflict, perhaps even instigate racial warfare. In a number of cities, white supremacist mobs attacked the Freedom Riders with clubs and chains, feet and fists.

But white racists were not the only critics of the Freedom Rides. Even CORE's ostensible allies charged that the protests—violating southern Jim Crow laws—were polarizing and damaging to the cause of racial equality. Those critics included President John F. Kennedy, who worked behind the scenes, unsuccessfully, to bring the Freedom Rides to a halt. In a moment of incivility in the Oval Office, Kennedy ranted to his aide, Harris Wofford, a well-known supporter of the southern freedom struggle: "Can't you get your god-damned friends off those buses...Stop them." In politer terms,

Kennedy, who was deeply suspicious of "passionate movements" and preferred technocratic solutions to social problems, urged civil rights activists
to be more "civil," which meant moving gradually by working through the
political system for change rather than taking to the streets (Arsenault 2006).

Kennedy's efforts to stop the Freedom Rides failed. Hundreds of activists
joined the protests for integrated interstate transportation—and in late fall
1961, they achieved their goal. The administration, fearful that the image
of the United States was being sullied by the ongoing civil rights protests,
tried to put a lid on the movement (Dudziak 2001). They encouraged civil
rights organizations to work behind the scenes. For Kennedy, civil rights
was a technical problem, best resolved through executive action (including
executive orders that forbade workplace discrimination and segregation in
new government-funded housing developments). He preferred that civil
rights leaders cooperate with government; he feared "passionate movements"
that would inflame the public (Stern 1992). But those efforts were only
partially successful. While executive branch officials consulted quietly with
civil rights leaders, protests escalated across the country. In places as diverse
as Birmingham, Selma, Detroit, and Philadelphia, civil rights activists took
to the streets, deploying tactics that pushed well beyond the boundaries of
what was considered civil. Many protestors, even those schooled in nonviolence, grew disaffected with what seemed to be the glacial progress of the
black freedom struggle (Segrue 2008).

Kennedy's reaction to the Freedom Rides—and the direction protests
took in the early and mid-1960s—fits uncomfortably with the wistful views
of the history of the civil rights movement that prevail today, a half century
later. In one of the more influential recent arguments on behalf of civility
in political discourse, Yale law professor Stephen Carter offered a lesson in
the history of the civil rights movement: Protestors were "loving" and "civil
in their dissent against a system willing and ready to destroy them." Martin
Luther King Jr., argues Carter, "understood that uncivil dialogue serves no
democratic function" (1998, 24) Carter's interpretation is reinforced in
popular memories of the civil rights struggle. King is cast as a unifier, not
a divider, someone who used the power of morality to call America to its
founding principles of equality and opportunity. The nonviolent protestors
of groups like CORE and the Southern Christian Leadership Conference are
cast as moderates, in contrast to those militants like Malcolm X and Stokely
Carmichael who called for militant self-defense and revolution.

Such binaristic accounts of the black freedom struggle distort the past.
Civil rights activists deployed a wide range of tactics that spanned a broad

spectrum of civility. Some called for moral suasion and education, and fashioned high-minded appeals to religious and political tradition. Others worked through the legislative process, deploying experts and lobbyists to make a case for civil rights laws. Still others took more adversarial positions, mounting lawsuits and fighting for justice in the courts. Some of the most visible activists and their organizations engaged in picketing, mass marches, and protests, which ranged from informational to disruptive. Coercive tactics—boycotts, strikes, and civil disobedience—proliferated at the end of the Depression, during World War II, and especially in early and mid-1960s. And most controversially, some called for disruption, violence, and disorder, or used the threat of disorder as tools to win concessions from the powerful. Very few of these tactics were, even in the broadest sense of the term, civil (Sugrue 2008, Kryder 2000, Joseph 2006).

Each of these tactics had staunch advocates: pro-civil rights leaders believed in the power of the pulpit. Advocates of nonviolence believed in eschewing the tactics of the oppressor. Revolutionaries called for the violent overthrow of Jim Crow. But most civil rights activists were not purists. They were improvisational, adopting different tactics at different times, aware of the opportunities of each strategy, but also their limits. Moral suasion and dialogue could build sympathy for the movement, but what about the vast majority of whites who were indifferent or openly hostile to the demands of civil rights? Changing how people talked about race did not necessarily lead to changes in how they behaved. And protests alone could raise consciousness about injustices, but litigation and legislation were necessary to spur change. Court decisions and laws were not, however, self-enforcing. To get public authorities to carry out laws often necessitated further protest and, often, the threat of coercion and disruption. Taking the movement to the streets could just as easily alienate potential supporters as win sympathy. Violence and disruption might force recalcitrant public officials to make changes in service of restoring order, but they might also lead to retribution and retaliation. The struggle for racial equality progressed when activists mixed these tactics—when they combined the civil and the disruptive, when they worked to change hearts and minds but also to transform institutions, often by any means necessary. The most significant gains of the civil rights movement were almost always the result of multi-tactic activism.

The possibilities and limits of persuasion

On the civil side of the spectrum were those advocates of racial equality who appealed to the intellect and conscience of white Americans. In his 1944 book, *An American Dilemma* (arguably the most influential social scientific account of race relations in the United States ever written), Gunnar Myrdal wrote that "*The Negro problem,*" all in italics, "*is a problem in the heart of the American. It is there that the interracial tension has its focus. It is there that the decisive struggle goes on.*" American values, which he called "boundless, idealistic aspirations" of "the American Creed," stood in sharp contrast to "personal and local interests; economic, social, and sexual jealousies; considerations of community prestige and conformity; group prejudice against particular persons or types of people; and all sorts of miscellaneous wants, impulses, and habits." At the core of Myrdal's book is a fundamentally optimistic view of the American people. Americans are fundamentally "moralistic" and deeply "rationalistic." These traits, in Myrdal's words, were the "glory of the nation, its youthful strength, perhaps the salvation of mankind." The challenge to solving America's Negro problem would be to appeal to the moral sentiments and the reason of ordinary white Americans. Faced with evidence of the appalling gap between the national rhetoric of equality and opportunity—and duly chastened by appeals to their sense of ethics and justice—white Americans would jettison their prejudices (1944, xlii, xliii). Myrdal tapped a deep root in the American social reform tradition— a faith in human perfectibility. If people were fundamentally good then moral suasion—appeals to their deepest, most humane sentiments—could fundamentally transform society.

The dominant current in civil rights activism in the postwar years—like Myrdal—emphasized moral suasion. Through school curricula, sermons, films, and popular articles, advocates of racial dialogue attempted to appeal to the "American creed" of equality. Education and persuasion, in their view, would lead to racial equality. But it quickly became clear that changing attitudes or, more superficially, the tone of racial discourse, had limits. Public opinion (at least as measured by surveys and polls) shifted decisively on matters of race between the 1940s and 1960s. Overt expressions of racial prejudice lost their legitimacy. But patterns of racial segregation changed very slowly, especially in the realms of housing and education. In the North, patterns of racial segregation in the housing market barely changed at all between the 1920s and the 1990s (Massey and Denton 1993). Despite a liberalization in attitudes, federal housing policy, local real estate practices, and whites' unwillingness to live in communities with more than a handful of minority residents meant large-scale segregation. And the shift in attitudes had unanticipated consequences. Large numbers of whites—and political leaders—couched their opposition to civil rights legislation (such as laws forbidding discrimination in employment and housing) by professing that they were colorblind. That rhetoric became so widespread by the mid-1960s that even many of the most vocal opponents of civil rights legislation argued that racial equality could not be legislated—only reasoned dialogue and discourse, prayer and reflection, would lead to a shift in attitudes and behavior over time, or that segregation was the result of the neutral working of the market (Lassiter 2009).

The limits of civility were abundantly clear in places like Greensboro, North Carolina, the subject of historian William Chafe's classic book, *Civilities and Civil Rights* (1980). There in the 1950s and early 1960s, civic leaders eschewed the blunt tactics of massive resistance to court-ordered desegregation. Greensboro had long prided itself on its enlightened racial politics; white politicians were disdainful of "rednecks" who used violence to maintain the system of Jim Crow. When the Supreme Court ruled in *Brown v. Board of Education* (1954) that racially separate schools were unequal and unconstitutional, Greensboro's school board—unlike many in the South—agreed to comply with the case. But they did so through token integration. The city's schools remained almost completely segregated for more than a decade after *Brown*—even as local leaders prided themselves on their enlightened policy. When younger black activists expressed exasperation at the glacial pace of change, Greensboro's ostensibly liberal white elite denounced them for pushing too far, too fast. Civility played out differently in Greenville, Mississippi, but it too was bound up with the maintenance of the status quo. Of Greenville, as historian Joseph Crespino (2007) writes, "manners were always intimately tied up with the operation of Jim Crow." There white leaders advocated civility as a "last ditch effort to stave off a new system of politics," choosing to distance themselves from white supremacist violence when it proved counterproductive. In both cases, as different as they were, civility served the cause of white supremacy.

The failures of gradualism and the limits of suasion were also visible in high relief north of the Mason-Dixon line. Northerners prided themselves on their liberality on civil rights matters; they viewed racial inequality as a distinctively Southern problem, the strange fruit of the region's peculiar institution. And Northerners had been the key targets of postwar efforts at moral suasion. Churchgoers in most mainstream Protestant congregations had been fed a steady diet of anti-prejudice education. On annual Brotherhood Sundays, ministers preached of the equality of humanity in the eyes of God. In synagogues, Jews were taught to analogize their own history of racial oppression with that of African Americans. And key Catholic intellectuals and members of the hierarchy joined calls for racial justice. Those religious efforts were effective, particularly at changing racial discourse. By the early 1960s, nearly three quarters of northern whites accepted—in principle—sending their children to school with blacks or having a black neighbor. Just twenty years earlier, nearly three quarters of whites would not accept even a single black neighbor (Sheatsley 1966). It became increasingly taboo to use overt racist language in public. But that shift in attitudes did not lead naturally into changed practices. Northern metropolitan areas grew more segregated by race, just as racial discourse was shifting. Even if whites believed that they were no longer prejudiced, they voted with their feet and left neighborhoods and schools that attracted more than a token number of blacks. Racial advancement—in housing, employment, education—came very slowly.

Civil rights leaders grew increasingly aware of the limits of civility and dialogue, even if few gave up on the efforts to change hearts and minds. By the late 1950s, protestors, both North and South, began to deploy more coercive techniques, including mass marches, demonstrations, civil disobedience, and, increasingly, disruption. Black parents led boycotts of separate and unequal schools, especially in the North. Students in Southern towns, even in those places that considered themselves progressive, like Greensboro and Atlanta, challenged segregation at lunch counters and theaters through civil disobedience. A growing number of blacks called for armed self-defense against segregationists. When the nonviolent Freedom Rides arrived in Monroe, North Carolina, for example, they were protected from angry white mobs by a security force of gun wielding black men, organized by Robert F. Williams, a former NAACP activist who later penned a famous book called *Negroes with Guns* (Tyson 2001). As protests grew more militant, civil rights advocates did not always agree on tactics—some called for nonviolence, others called for self-defense and revolt, and still others argued that all forms of protest would be counterproductive and that education and persuasion should come first. For these activists who built on the strategy of Gandhian nonviolence, protest was in part intended to reveal the brutality that undergirded Jim Crow. But most protestors—Gandhian or not—saw protest as a form of wielding power and saw coercion as necessary to change. Social gains would not result solely or primarily from polite dialogue: they would result from pressure on the system.

That combination of dialogue and disruption animated both CORE and King. From CORE's origins in the early 1940s through the mid-1960s, its most committed members intended their protests to be acts of moral suasion.

Black and white sitting together in restaurants, sharing swimming pools, and sitting side by side on buses would serve as examples of the interracial beloved community that they hoped to create. From their very first protests—at segregated restaurants in Chicago during World War II—through the Freedom Rides and open housing protests of the Kennedy years, CORE members believed in engaging with their opponents with respect and dignity. King—trained in the Social Gospel and in the art of preaching—also believed in the power of moral suasion. He used the power of the pulpit to persuade churchgoers of the injustice of Jim Crow. And he used his compelling rhetoric to mobilize Americans against racial injustice and economic inequality in places as diverse as Montgomery, Alabama, and Chicago, Illinois. King was particularly effective in using the news media—especially television—as a tribune to carry the message of racial equality to a wide audience. Dialogue mattered (Meier and Rudwick 1973, Jackson 2007).

But fostering dialogue was only one tactic, only one weapon of the weak. And it was not always the most effective. By the early 1960s, nonviolent activists in the freedom struggle engaged in protests whose primary goal was not to spark dialogue; rather they intended to provoke violent retaliation. The most illustrative case was the mass protests in Birmingham, Alabama, in the spring of 1963. When Martin Luther King Jr. and the Southern Christian Leadership Conference planned demonstrations in Birmingham, they chose their target fully aware of the risks that the protests entailed. A deeply segregated city with a long history of racial violence, Birmingham was defended by the notoriously vicious city commissioner, Eugene "Bull" Connor. King and the SCLC knew full well that a confrontation with Connor's forces would result in bloodshed. King's critics (including some sympathetic with the goals of the movement) tried to discourage the protests, aware that the cost of provoking Commissioner Bull Connor and his police would be high. Moderate church and civic leaders argued that mass demonstrations would only harden white resistance to civil rights. King's decision to enlist schoolchildren in the protest was especially controversial. There was nothing civil about pitting the young and vulnerable against a phalanx of armed law enforcement officials. The resulting clashes—peaceful protestors attacked by police dogs and blasted by fire hoses—were broadcast globally. It was the very incivility of the Birmingham protests—and the violent reaction to them—that became a turning point in the history of the black freedom struggle in the United States (Eskew 1997, McWhorter 2001).

In the aftermath of the protests, King aimed some of his harshest words toward advocates of civility. In *Letter from a Birmingham Jail*, he wrote that

"I have almost reached the regrettable conclusion that the Negro's great stumbling block in his stride toward freedom is not the White Citizen's Counciler or the Ku Klux Klanner, but the white moderate, who is more devoted to 'order' than to justice; who prefers a negative peace which is the absence of tension to a positive peace which is the presence of justice; who constantly says: 'I agree with you in the goal you seek, but I cannot agree with your methods of direct action'; who paternalistically believes he can set the timetable for another man's freedom; who lives by a mythical concept of time and who constantly advises the Negro to wait for a 'more convenient season.' Shallow understanding from people of good will is more frustrating than absolute misunderstanding from people of ill will. Lukewarm acceptance is much more bewildering than outright rejection" (King 1963).

The spring protests in Birmingham spurred a wave of protests nationwide, many of them even more disruptive (indeed, just after King left Birmingham, rioters took to the city's downtown shopping district, breaking windows and looting stores, expressing their outrage at the intransigence of Jim Crow). By the end of the year, thousands of protests had erupted throughout the country. Many of them were not particularly civil. In Philadelphia, civil rights protestors turned up with angry dogs (in a symbolic inversion of the Birmingham protests) and remade the anthem "We Shall Overcome" into an ominous chant, with rolled up newspapers serving as percussion: "We...shall...over...come/ we...shall...over...come." Birmingham-style mini-riots broke out in places as diverse as Rochester and New Rochelle, New York, anticipating the long hot summers that would punctuate the remainder of the 1960s. Observers declared 1963 the year of the "Negro Revolt" (Sugrue 2008).

Even at iconic civil rights events in 1963, the threat of disruption loomed large. CORE protests against unequal education in Chicago began as peaceful demonstrations but turned violent. Demonstrators against workplace discrimination in Philadelphia and New York deployed increasingly disruptive tactics, including blockading construction sites, chaining themselves to cranes, and clashing with law enforcement officials. In Englewood, New Jersey, protests against school segregation included (often uneasily) members of the local NAACP chapter, former Freedom Riders, and members of the Nation of Islam. Police forces around the United States began purchasing riot gear and preparing for what they feared was an impending race war. And civil rights leaders—even the most moderate—capitalized on the threat of disorder to demand legislation.

Ultimately fears of mass disruption, of escalating violence and domestic strife, led the Kennedy administration to move decisively. On June 11, the president addressed the nation on the "fires of frustration and discord that are burning in every city, North and South, where legal remedies are not at hand. Redress is sought in the streets, in demonstrations, parades and protests which create tensions and threaten violence and threaten lives." It was, the president stated, "a time of domestic crisis." Speaking to his hope that social problems could be solved without protest, he made the point baldly: "It is better to settle these matters in the courts than on the streets" (Kennedy 1963). Later that month, the president tasked administration officials with drafting sweeping civil rights legislation, laying the groundwork for landmark 1964 legislation. Dialogue and moral suasion laid the groundwork for the passage of civil rights laws, but disruption and the threat of disorder were even more important catalysts to change.

The possibilities and limits of disruption

In the second half of the 1960s, civil rights protests of all varieties escalated. In the North, followers of Malcolm X often joined protests against segregated schools and workplaces. By the mid-1960s, many CORE chapters repudiated the long-standing vision of the beloved community with demands for black self-determination. In the South, disaffected members of the Student Non-Violent Coordinating Committee advocated self-defense. In 1966, when Student Non-Violent Coordinating Committee leader Stokely Carmichael uttered the two words "Black Power" at an Alabama protest, alarmed observers suggested that nonviolent tactics were being supplanted by a dangerous militancy. Media attention turned to the most inflammatory advocates of revolution, most notably the Black Panther Party (Joseph 2006). But even as militants dominated the evening news, advocates of moral suasion, nonviolence, and integration did not fade—indeed they were at their peak of influence. Building on the strategies of King and the SCLC and allying with them, the new, interracial welfare rights movement engaged in a mix of protest, civil disobedience, lobbying, and litigation. The open housing movement—which attempted to break down discrimination in the housing market—reached its peak of influence in the late 1960s. Hundreds of open housing groups—many working closely with church and civic groups— worked in the late 1960s to foster dialogue and to persuade homeowners and realtors to accept the principle of nondiscrimination in housing. And the National Association for the Advancement of Colored People (NAACP) reached its peak post-World War II membership at the end of the 1960s, when it dwarfed the more telegenic black power movement. As in the prior years, the spectrum of activism ranged from moral suasion to self-defense, from dialogue to disruption.

But in the post-1966 period, the mix of strategies changed, largely because of discontent from below with the limitations of legislation and litigation and the gradualism of change. In the summer of 1967, hundreds of thousands of African Americans took to the streets, protesting and, increasingly, looting and burning. Big cities like Detroit and Newark erupted in some of the most violent civil disorders in the century, but so too did many smaller towns, among them Plainfield, New Jersey, and even little Wadesboro, North Carolina. Altogether more than 160 cities and towns burned in the long hot summers. The urban uprisings or riots were anything but civil, but behind them (as with previous protests) were demands for recognition (National Advisory Commission on Civil Disorders 1968). More so than many previous protests, the uprisings revealed the limits of incivility, the dangers of disruption. To be sure, the riots had significant consequences in the short run: local elected officials and business leaders, many of whom had ignored black demands for economic justice, responded speedily. Business and civic groups spent hundreds of millions of dollars in community development efforts, especially in the biggest riot-torn cities like Newark and Detroit. City officials—looking to buy off future discontent—moved aggressively to hire blacks in visible (but still mostly white) positions in law enforcement. And the Johnson administration channeled millions to cities through the model cities program. Even Nixon launched a program to spur "black capitalism" and greatly expanded funding for black entrepreneurs through the Office of Minority Business Enterprise. Cynics dismissed these efforts as "riot insurance," but the very term suggested the efficacy of what historian Robert Fogelson (1971) called "violence as protest." But the riots also had negative consequences—their incivility and violence fueled demands for law and order, expanded police power, and resulted in more aggressive incarceration policies (Katz 2011).

Whether in Birmingham in 1963 or Newark in 1967, the struggle for racial equality was characterized by a mix of civility and incivility. What is clear is that neither—alone—could be an effective vehicle for social change. Change depended on both. The history of the black freedom struggle offers abundant evidence of the limits of civility. Dialogue and persuasion were necessary—but far from sufficient—to accomplish the goal of racial equality. Changing hearts and minds—and even changing laws—seldom changed society quickly or decisively. Those changes resulted as much from fears of disorder, than from actual transgression or the threat of it. Threatening established power relationships and undermining the structures of inequality in the civil rights era was inherently uncivil. Looking back at the 1960s through the prism of contemporary debates about what is civil and what is not, overlooks in the end the fact that to those whose power (economic, social, racial) was threatened by civil rights, the whole struggle was uncivil. From J. Edgar Hoover's denunciation of Martin Luther King Jr. as the "most dangerous Negro in America" to oft-repeated concerns that "outside agitators" were responsible for pickets, protests, and riots alike, to inflammatory critiques of groups as diverse as CORE, the SCLC, and the Black Panthers as "un-American" and destructive—all are a reminder that civility is in the eye of the beholder. And when the beholder wants to maintain an unequal status quo, picketers, protestors, and preachers alike are uncivil as much because of their message as their methods.

References

Arsenault, Raymond. 2006. *Freedom Riders: 1961 and the Struggle for Racial Justice.* New York: Oxford University Press.

Carter, Stephen L. 1998. *Civility: Manners, Morals, and the Etiquette of Democracy.* New York: Basic Books.

Chafe, William Henry. 1980. *Civilities and Civil Rights: Greensboro, North Carolina, and the Black Struggle for Freedom.* New York: Oxford University Press.

Crespino, Joseph. 2007. "Civilities and Civil Rights in Mississippi." In *Manners and Southern History: Essays,* edited by Ted Ownby, 114-136. Jackson: University Press of Mississippi.

Dudziak, Mary. 2001. *Cold War Civil Rights: Race and the Image of American Democracy.* Princeton: Princeton University Press.

Eskew, Glenn T. 1997. *But for Birmingham: The Local and National Movements in the Civil Rights Struggle.* Chapel Hill: University of North Carolina Press.

Fogelson, Robert M. 1971. *Violence as Protest: A Study of Riots and Ghettos.* Garden City, NY: Doubleday.

Jackson, Thomas F. 2007. *From Civil Rights to Human Rights: Martin Luther King, Jr., and the Struggle for Economic Justice.* Philadelphia: University of Pennsylvania Press.

Joseph, Peniel E. 2006. *Waiting 'Til the Midnight Hour: A Narrative History of Black Power in America.* New York: Henry Holt.

Katz, Michael B. 2011. *Why Don't American Cities Burn?* Philadelphia: University of Pennsylvania Press.

Kennedy, John Fitzgerald. 1963. Address on Civil Rights, June 11. millercenter.org/president/speeches/detail/3375.

King, Martin Luther, Jr. 1963. "Letter from Birmingham Jail." April 16. mlk-kpp01.stanford.edu/index.php/encyclopedia/documentsentry/annotated_letter_from_birmingham.

Kryder, Daniel. 2000. *Divided Arsenal: Race and the American State During World War II.* New York: Cambridge University Press.

Lassiter, Matthew D. 2009. "De Jure/De Facto Segregation: The Long Shadow of a National Myth." In *The Myth of Southern Exceptionalism,* edited by Matthew D. Lassiter and Joseph Crespino, 25-48. New York: Oxford University Press.

Massey, Douglas S., and Nancy A. Denton. 1993. *American Apartheid: Race and the Making of the Underclass*. Cambridge: Harvard University Press.

McWhorter, Diane. 2001. *Carry Me Home: Birmingham, Alabama, the Climactic Battle of the Civil Rights Revolution*. New York: Simon and Schuster.

Meier, August, and Elliott Rudwick. 1973. *CORE: A Study in the Civil Rights Movement, 1942-1968*. Urbana: University of Illinois Press.

Myrdal, Gunnar. 1944. *An American Dilemma: The Negro Problem and Modern Democracy*. New York: Harper Brothers. Italics with the exception of the first line.

National Advisory Commission on Civil Disorders. 1968. *Report*. Washington, DC: U.S. Government Printing Office.

Sheatsley, Paul. 1966. "White Attitudes toward the Negro." *Daedalus* 95(1): 217-238.

Stern, Mark. 1992. *Calculating Visions: Kennedy, Johnson, and Civil Rights*. New Brunswick: Rutgers University Press.

Sugrue, Thomas J. 2008. *Sweet Land of Liberty: The Forgotten Struggle for Civil Rights in the North*. New York: Random House.

Tyson, Timothy. 2001. *Radio Free Dixie: Robert F. Williams and the Roots of Black Power*. Chapel Hill: University of North Carolina Press.

II
Religion

Faith in Religion, Civility, and Democracy

Matthew Avery Sutton, Washington State University

||||||||||||||||||||||||||||||||||||||||||||||||||||||||||||||||||||||||||||||||||||||||||||||||||||||||||||||||||||||||||||||||||||||||||

In recent years, the National Endowment for the Humanities (NEH) has sought to better understand the relationship between civility and democracy. According to the NEH, "Civility has always served as a keystone in the American experiment...Civility involves our responsibilities to each other as citizens and as members of civil society." Many scholars have argued that freedom of religion and the separation of church and state are also vitally important foundations upon which the United States was built. Furthermore, religion, like civility, "involves our responsibilities to each other as citizens and as members of civil society" (2011).

As scholars in various fields have explored the relationship between civility and democracy, both in the nation's past and in contemporary society, a number of key issues have emerged. The following three essays analyze the ways in which religion and civility relate to each other. Among the most important questions they address are: Have civility and religion been mutually reinforcing in the American past (and/or in modern American culture) or are they working at cross purposes? What is the relationship between religion and democracy? How do religions function in a democracy and how do they influence the civility or incivility of the larger society? Is civility defined differently by various religions? How should we understand the relationship between exclusivist religious claims and pluralistic communities? Three of the nation's leading scholars of American religion, Amanda Porterfield, Paul Boyer, and Wade Clark Roof, approach these questions from a variety of perspectives.

Porterfield argues that the founding fathers and mothers of the United States had a deep, historically-grounded view of civility. For them, "civility meant active devotion to and willingness to take responsibility for the common good." They believed that "as a marker of virtuous personality, civility involved the ability to rise above narrow self-interest and partisanship."

The founders presumed that "civility ultimately derived and depended on a preexisting purpose for the world," which came from religion. In subsequent decades and then centuries, however, fewer and fewer Americans agreed with the founders on this point. In modern times, divine cosmology and providential courses of history no longer serve as the foundation for civil society. According to recent polls, although many Americans still ascribe to traditional (essentially Protestant) views of God, increasing numbers of Americans do not. Furthermore, the state and federal courts have gone to great lengths to limit Protestant expressions of faith in the public sphere and to protect the rights of non-Christian minorities (Kosmin and Keysar 2009).

What has been the result? According to Porterfield, on the one hand religious conservatives have expressed deep frustration over efforts to ban religion from American public life. Religious liberals, on the other hand, have "appealed to an ideal of religious pluralism that promotes the voices of religious minorities as an expression of American democracy and seeks ecumenical cooperation as the epitome of democratic civility." Neither approach is satisfactory. Porterfield argues that the conservative approach is no longer realistic—the days of Protestant hegemony are long gone. But the problem with celebrating pluralism is liberals' failure to take seriously religion's violent aspects. She asserts that, "because of its capacity for deep emotional resonance, openness to multiple meanings, and special appeal to charismatic individuals, bullies, and demagogues, religion does not provide stable ground for either democracy or civility. While civil democracy requires freedom of religion, the reverse does not hold. Religion does not require civil democracy and may often threaten it." So, for Porterfield, is there a solution? Yes and no. "Rather than enlisting in one side or the other of the partisan war over which approach to religion should prevail, the time has come," she concludes, "to agree that the ground has shifted and better understand the emotional and political forces working within that shift and resistance to it."

Like Porterfield, Boyer also begins his discussion of religion, civility, and democracy by explaining how the concept of civility has functioned in the American past. Civility, he explains, refers to "structural relationships" defined historically by "equal justice before the law, a democratic form of government, tolerance of diverse views and beliefs, and a general equality of condition." Civility is not really about good manners or good relationships but about larger structural forces.

Once Boyer identifies the nature of civility, he raises the question: "Surveying the full span of United States history, has religion furthered or impeded civility?" His answer: religion has done both. Abolitionists, social gospel leaders, and civil rights activists have all sought the "preservation of a civil society" and they have worked to overcome "the racial, ethnic, and class barriers that always threaten to fragment the commons into hostile, mutually distrustful enclaves." But this, of course, is not the whole story. Boyer also cites examples such as the Know Nothing party and the Ku Klux Klan to demonstrate how religion has fostered incivility, promoted negative stereotypes about competing faiths, and worked for destructive social legislation.

Turning to the present, Boyer explains that religion, civility, and democracy continue to have a mixed relationship. Many Americans have been calling for and celebrating a more diverse and tolerant civil society, while exclusivist forms of fundamentalist religion have been simultaneously attracting large numbers of converts. In particular, he focuses on the ways in which the preoccupation of significant numbers of Americans on an imminent apocalypse shapes their views of civil society. For them, a "civil" society is neither a worthwhile goal nor a possible achievement. Instead, the world is broken down into good and evil, saved and sinner. In this sense, the present is very much like the past in that religion is a complicated category that individuals and groups can use for many different ends. He concludes that "any serious discussion of religion in contemporary culture and politics must take into account the millions of citizens who bring to the public sphere an unwavering allegiance to religious dogmas that trump all other considerations, and an apocalyptic vision of human history as a divinely ordained drama that is rushing inexorably toward its final climax."

Roof focuses directly on the ways in which civility and religion are connected and also on how the relationship between the two is undergoing significant changes. He begins by invoking sociologist Emile Durkheim to argue that it is essential that we understand what holds a nation together, what creates social and cultural solidarity. Like Porterfield and Boyer, he argues that for much of American history, Protestant culture served as the glue that bound the nation. In more recent years, however, increasing numbers of Americans have challenged Protestant hegemony. Secularists, those of other faiths, and moderate-minded Protestants and Catholics argue that the nation's foundations lie in "laws and customs such as the separation of church and state, voluntary faith, the sacred quality of conscience, equality, and freedom of religion or no religion—as stated in, or inspired by, the First Amendment to the Constitution." The tension between those who hold this view and those who look back to the days of Protestant dominance in the 19th century has not been resolved.

Next, Roof turns to the ways in which the divide between those he calls conservatives—who look to Protestant faith to shape and define the culture—and those he calls progressives—those who view laws and customs as fundamental—are increasingly seeing their differences played out in the political sphere. As a result, "civility is extended to others, or limited to them, in what amounts typically to the use of political weaponry as a means of expressing religious conviction and action." Finally, Roof concludes by arguing that civility is not about achieving consensus but about respecting the differing views of others. He argues that Americans need to "engage the other, to listen, and to respect those with whom" they disagree. Civil debate, he further explains, "involves trying to understand better where the other is coming from, and indirectly, where we are coming from when we disagree with one another. We must ask not just how our visions of a good society differ, but also why, and how they can be enhanced through conversation. In the practice of civility," he concludes, "might we even come to recognize that our own views are better understood even by ourselves—perhaps actually enriched—through dialogue?"

These three essays address a number of important themes. The authors all believe that Americans' notions of civility are tightly linked to their understandings of religion. Therefore, if we want to understand civility in the United States, we must also better understand how religion functions and serves to shape it. However, the close relationship between civility and democracy has created a number of problems. For roughly the first 100 years of the nation's history, Protestants so dominated the culture that they were able to define the nature of that civility and exclude those with whom they disagreed. Things have since changed. All three authors emphasize the growing religious diversity of the American population, and all three discuss the ways in which this growing diversity has created substantial tensions between those who long for the return of Protestant hegemony and those who seek new foundations upon which to build notions of civility and the public good. These tensions in part fuel the culture wars and have produced growing partisan divides. Where we—where the nation—goes from here is yet to be determined. But whatever paths Americans choose as they redefine the relationship between civility and democracy, it is clear that religion will be an essential component.

References

Kosmin, Barry A., and Ariela Keysar. March 2009. "American Religious Identification Survey (ARIS 2008)." commons.trincoll.edu/aris/files/2011/08/ARIS_Report_2008.pdf.
NEH (National Endowment for the Humanities). 2011. "Bridging Cultures: Implementation Grants for Public Programs on 'Civility and Democracy' or 'The Muslim World and the Humanities.'" neh.gov/grants/public/bridging-cultures-implementation-grants-public-programs-civility-and-democracy.

Religion's Role in Contestations over American Civility

Amanda Porterfield, Florida State University

IIIIIIIIIIIIIIIIIIIIIIIIIIIIIIIIIIIIIIIIIIIIIIIIIIIIIIIIIIIIIIIIIIIIIIIIIIIIIIIIIIIIIIIIIIIIIIIIIIIIIIIIIIIIIIIIIIIIIIIIIIIIIIIIIIIIII

Since the founding of the United States, religious ideals have contributed to conceptions of citizenship and civility. But American political life has persistently fallen far short of these ideals, and religious leaders have often expressed dismay about the corrupt state of the nation. Contributing to chronic feelings of disappointment, suspicion, and betrayal as well as to idealized conceptions of public life, religion has provoked incivility by amplifying public frustration and by denouncing persons deemed morally unfit, even as it has also contributed to conceptions and practices of civility. Questions about the legitimacy and utility of religion have only heightened this two-way pull, escalating animosity about America's capitulation to the forces of darkness while also prompting new religious efforts to preserve religion as an essential contributor to civil society.

At the time of the founding of the American republic, conceptions of civility derived from a combination of different sources, including Renaissance depictions of civic virtue in the ancient republics of Greece and Rome, the federal covenant theology of English Puritanism, and the social contract theories of John Locke and Jean Jacques Rousseau. Against the idealistic foil of these sources, considerable anxiety existed about the stability of a government founded in revolution and the overthrow of monarchy. Aggressive land speculation and Indian removal along with canny strategies for the protection and growth of slavery fed animosity toward government control and only deepened anxiety about the integrity and stability of the new American republic. Leading men developed civic institutions that, to some extent, served their own interests as landholders, and in many cases slave owners, and the practice of civility enabled them to do so. The erection of a new federal government institutionalized deep disagreements among these men, and many of these disagreements touched on the relationship between religion and government. These disagreements have never been resolved, but only evolved over time, making religion and its relationship to government an ongoing point of contention—and occasion for incivility.

Though the founders disagreed on many political and religious points, their notions of civility coincided in agreement that, as a marker of virtuous personality, civility involved the ability to rise above narrow self-interest and partisanship (Pocock 2003, 518). This agreement about what civility entailed worked against forthright expressions of ambition and open admissions of self-interest, especially in public figures, thus contributing to the fiction of disinterested benevolence as well as to the smooth conduct of business. In 1788, no one represented this standard of virtuous personality and capacity for public leadership more perfectly than the wealthy landowner George Washington. Thus in a letter to Henry Lee on September 22, 1788, shortly before his election as the first President of the United States, Washington denied having any ambition for public office, vowing that if accused of ambition, he would not let such low opinion of his intentions stand in the way of duty to God, country, and conscience. "Though I prize, as I ought, the good opinion of my fellow citizens; yet, if I know myself, I would not seek or retain popularity at the expense of one social duty or moral virtue." Washington's finely balanced combination of self-respect and nonpartisan transcendence of self interest was precisely what his electors wanted. "While doing what my conscience informed me was right, as it respected my God, my Country and myself," Washington explained, "I could despise all the party clamor and unjust censure, which must be expected from some, whose personal enmity might be occasioned by their hostility to the government" (Washington 1939, 97-98).

Working against the fear that their republican form of government might descend into anarchy, the men who drafted the U.S. Constitution worked to erect a government of laws rather than men, and a system of checks and balances that would stabilize their enterprise in lieu of monarchical authority and its claim to divine legitimacy. They were keenly aware that the government they were erecting was a work of human art and thus of an order different from the order of nature, and different in kind from a government established through the will of God, as monarchy claimed to be (Slauter 2009). At the same time, however, they made assumptions about moral virtue and its implications for civility that were rooted, in their minds, in metaphysical assumptions, many of which rested on beliefs about God. Thus the new secular order these men brought into being coexisted with an ideal of public leadership and an understanding of nature and humanity that depended on metaphysical ideals that were more or less equivalent to religious principles. They disagreed about the nature and implications of metaphysical order, but not about its existence. A shared belief in a natural order to things, however much its details were disputed, complemented belief in civility and virtuous, nonpartisan leadership. Both sets of ideals papered over contentious and messy realities.

The process that resulted in ratification of the U.S. Constitution was conflicted, but for all their disputes, the participants in this process shared the hope that the civility they aimed for was intended by God, and that it would flourish in the republic they founded. The founders held different opinions about God's attributes and modes of operation, but they never disputed that the world was created by an intelligent force, or that this force had established an order to nature that stood in the background of their own creative endeavor, lending tacit support.

While God does not appear in the Constitution except in its conclusion (Article VII) in "the year of our Lord one thousand seven hundred and Eighty seven," none of the people who debated constitutional law and participated in the Constitutional Convention would have contested James Madison's statement two years earlier that, "Before any man can be considered a member of civil society, he must be considered as a subject of the Governor of the Universe" (Madison [1785] 2003, 64). For supporters of the U.S. Constitution in the 1780s, all forms of government existed within a larger cosmology of universal government to which all people were subject. This pair of metaphysical principles grounding the Constitution would not be disputed until much later—that there was a divine Governor of the Universe, and that God imposed a primary obligation to himself upon individuals.

Thus beneath a host of specific disagreements about Jesus, miracles, and how the Bible should be interpreted, participants in the construction of American government all presumed that civility ultimately derived and depended on a preexisting purpose for the world. While acknowledging the danger of political factions and bowing to the power of competing interests, participants in the constitutional process all believed that God had created the world, that each individual was obligated to God, however poorly people understood or fulfilled that obligation, and that moral conscience involved obligation to others, however limited or small the circle.

In erecting a republican government built upon this understanding of human nature, participants in the constitutional debates hoped that the representatives selected to serve in the government would be, as Madison wrote in the Federalist Papers #10, "a chosen body of citizens, whose wisdom may best discern the true interest of their country and whose patriotism and love of justice will be least likely to sacrifice it to temporary or partial considerations." Moral sentiment, Madison and other founders believed, would lead the people's representatives to govern in the best interests of the people, however imperfectly. Rejecting monarchy and the stability associated with the divine right of kings, the men who ratified the U.S. Constitution banked on this moral sentiment to produce civility. Their boldness in doing so rested on confidence in God's existence and governance of the world. Americans today operate within the system of government they devised, but without as much underlying agreement about God, and civility's dependence on his existence, that the founders shared.

Assumptions of moral order embedded in the universe, exerting force on individuals, has generated expectations of civility that have constrained anti-social activity and reinforced tendencies to cooperation and mutual respect. At the same time, however, those same metaphysical assumptions have conflicted with the prevalence and incivility of partisan politics in American life, raising anxiety about divine support for American government. This anxiety has often erupted in apocalyptic rhetoric about America's loss of divine favor and need to regain it, and that rhetoric has subverted thoughtful analysis of how incivility emerges and what political interests it serves.

Long before citizens raised direct questions about the existence of God— and before state and federal courts found themselves in the unexpected position of having to protect nonbelievers from religious discrimination— partisans engaged in heated political conflict, defying the expectations of civility that had enabled ratification of the Constitution. In their defiance of civility, and demand that representatives in government see things their way, partisans did not hesitate to invoke religion. Thus in the 1790s, disputes over citizenship and equality, slavery, property rights, taxation, Indian affairs, and foreign policy became increasingly polarized as political activists on both sides of the growing partisan divide deployed religious rhetoric to defame their opposition. Religious invective fueled incivility in the early republic, establishing grooves for religion's role in public life that have continued to prove politically effective.

The partisan organization of American political culture thwarted the expectations of moral virtue and civic personality that the founders presumed the American system of government to be predicated upon. A defining characteristic of civic virtue, nonpartisanship disappeared in the bitter contest over Jefferson's election in 1800. Complicating matters further, instead of enabling the nonpartisan commitment to duty characteristic of civil virtue, political contestants deployed religion to dismantle it.

As an example of religion's role in the American tendency to partisan incivility, the summer before Jefferson's election, in an article "addressing those who…are not yet prepared to part with their Bible, their morals, or their God," Hartford's *Connecticut Courant* warned that Jefferson "dislikes all government, which is capable of affording protection and security to those who live under it" (Burleigh 1800, 3). On the other hand, pro-Jefferson republicans despised the sanctimony of Federalist elites who presumed to "lead all men to worship God in the presidential manner" (*Aurora* 1798). In Connecticut, they linked Federalist arrogance to religious corruption. One toast, "May true and undefiled religion pervade the whole earth, and that monster superstition become extinct," was followed by another, drunk to "The union of the States—May the links which form the chain be made of pure republican Gold so that the rust of aristocracy may not corrode and destroy it" (*American Mercury*).

Feeding the problem as much as providing remedy for it, many Americans have thought that the prevalence of incivility in American life demanded new infusions of religion, and more insistence on language about God. In the divided, highly politicized culture of American public life, religion has contributed to incivility, even as participants on both sides have held up their approaches to religion as prerequisites for civility. While proponents of secular government call for great tolerance for religious and non-religious points of view, and appeal to the prohibition against religious establishment they read into the First Amendment to the U.S. Constitution, religious conservatives decry what seems to them to be the moral relativism of their political opponents and its association with immorality and corruption.

Americans who argue that the United States was founded as a Christian nation, and that the country and its government have moved away from its moral and religious foundation, are not entirely wrong. Eight of the thirteen original states entered the union with some form of Protestant religious establishment mandating support for churches and requiring elected officials to swear religious oaths (Witte 2011, 57-58). Statesmen disagreed about whether Catholics, Jews, Quakers, Hindus, and Muslims should enjoy the same rights as Protestants, but even the great champion of religious freedom, Thomas Jefferson, did not argue that the state had an obligation to protect the rights of unbelievers. His infamous statement on religion—"It neither picks my pocket nor breaks my leg if my neighbor has one god or twenty gods"—was denounced by opponents as tantamount to acceptance of atheism, but in fact fell short of that mark, and was far removed from calling for a ban on religious expression in public places (Jefferson [1782] 1972, 159).

By 1833 all states had abandoned official establishments of particular Protestant churches. But a moral establishment of evangelical Christianity dominated American society in the 19th century, and Jeffersonian liberalism with respect to religious freedom was often denied. An 1811 decision in the New York Supreme Court asserted that Christianity was part of the common law inherited from England from which jurisprudence in all states had evolved. The New York case established a precedent that many other courts followed in prosecuting blasphemy and other behaviors offensive to Christian morality. In 1844, the U.S. Supreme Court upheld this line of reasoning in *Vidal v. Philadelphia*. Writing for the court, Joseph Story asserted that the "divine origin and truth" of Christianity was accepted, "and therefore it is not to be maliciously and openly reviled and blasphemed against, to the annoyance of believers or the injury of the public." The court also accepted the claim made by the defense attorney, Daniel Webster, that Christianity was the only true source of charity (Sehat 2011, 60-67).

Complaints that the religious ideals of American society have eroded are not without historical foundation. While the United States was not founded as an explicitly Christian nation, and early proponents of religious freedom resisted government intrusion in matters of individual conscience, the founders took for granted the existence of a divinely inspired moral order in the universe and built their notions of government and civility upon it. In the nineteenth century, Protestant evangelicals imbued American government with even greater moral force, reaching back to puritan notions of a people chosen by God to spread the gospel to all corners of the earth, and linking these millennial expectations of world redemption through Christianity to the territorial expansion and industrial development of the United States.

Religious conservatives today express profound discontent that, for many Americans, the world is no longer framed by a divine cosmology, much less by belief in a providential course of history disclosed through supernatural revelation. While polls indicate that most Americans still believe in God, and many of those believe that history is moving toward the end times described in scripture, a growing minority does not, and state and federal courts have upheld the right of that minority not to be subjected to religion. In an influential U.S. Supreme Court decision in 1971, the court ruled that religious schools could not receive state support. The religious schools in question were Catholic institutions receiving limited state funds for teaching secular subjects. The court banned that support in *Lemon v. Kurtzman*, with Justice Kennedy arguing that "a dedicated religious person, teaching at a school affiliated with his or her faith and operated to inculcate its tenets, will inevitably experience great difficulty in remaining religiously neutral." Building on such concern about "excess entanglement" between church and state in

1985, the U.S. Supreme Court decided in *Wallace v. Jaffree* to prohibit public schools from requiring moments of silence. In 2005 in *McCreary County v. ACLU*, the court forced the removal of a county courthouse display of the Ten Commandments (Witte 2011, 179).

Before her retirement in 2005, Justice Sandra Day O'Connor issued a series of influential opinions arguing for the rights of nonbelievers that reveal how ideas about civility have shifted away from assumptions that moral integrity must be rooted in personal obligation to God. Though she thought the state should protect the rights of citizens to express religious beliefs, she argued that the state could not make "adherence to religion relevant to a person's standing in the political community." Government support for religion was prohibited, she wrote in *Wallace v. Jaffee*, because it "sends a message to nonadherents that they are outsiders, not full members of the political community, and an accompanying message to adherents that they are insiders, favored members of the community" (Witte 2011, 181).

Questions about how much government should accommodate religion, and how far it should go in protecting the rights of nonbelievers, are far from settled. With O'Connor's departure from the court and the appointments of Justices John Roberts and Samuel Alito, religious conservatives have pressed for greater government accommodation of religion. For example, when a group of students and professors sued the Board of Trustees at Saddleback Community College in Orange County, California, for allowing the chairman of the board to make religious pronouncements at school events that students and professors were required to attend, the defendants mounted a well-funded and broad-ranging defense aimed at protecting the right to religious speech in public schools (*Karla Westphal v. Donald P. Wagner*, U.S. District Court for the Central District of California, Case No. 09-CV-8528).

While conservatives pushing back against restrictions on government accommodation of religion can exert powerful influence on legislation and judicial opinion, the dike of discrimination against nonbelievers has been breached. Defenders of public religious expression have been asked to show that that expression does not have the effect of ostracizing nonbelievers from public life, a criterion 19th-century litigants never had to meet. Well into the 20th century many states prohibited nonbelievers from testifying in courts, blasphemy laws denied free speech to atheists, and judges often linked civil government to the practice of Christianity (Sehat 2011, 68-69). Prior to *Lemon v. Kurtzman*, courts might assume government support for religion and protect the rights of religious minorities. Since that ruling in 1971, courts question government support more closely and protect the rights of nonreligious minorities.

While religious conservatives have been outraged by efforts to banish religion from American public life, religious liberals have appealed to an ideal of religious pluralism that promotes the voices of religious minorities as an expression of American democracy and seeks ecumenical cooperation as the epitome of democratic civility. As a leading proponent of religious pluralism, Diana Eck writes,

> Religious freedom has always given rise to religious diversity, and never has our diversity been more dramatic than it is today. This will require us to reclaim the deepest meaning of the very principles we cherish and to create a truly pluralist American society in which this great diversity is not simply tolerated but becomes the very source of our strength. (2001, 6)

For Eck, religion is what makes America great, and the growth of Hinduism, Buddhism, and Islam in the United States is a source of democratic revitalization. "As Americans, we need to see these signs of a new religious America and begin to think of ourselves anew in terms of them" (10). Mosques and churches sharing space and neighborliness, Hindu temples altering the skyline—these signs of inclusion are testament to America's greatness. Comparing religion in America to a brilliant piece of jazz, Eck makes religion the essence of American democracy and civility. "Learning to hear the musical lines of our neighbors," she writes, "their individual and magnificent interpretations of the themes of America's common covenants, is the test of cultural pluralism," a test she urges us to meet with enthusiastic participation (58-59).

But celebrations of religious pluralism exacerbate the tensions associated with the loss of firm religious grounding, even though its proponents strive for greater civic harmony through religious inclusiveness. Without denying the many cooperative efforts, charitable drives, and educational ventures that religious groups have sponsored in concert with other religious groups throughout American history, these efforts have often required compromises in belief and practice that Americans committed to rigorous interpretations of their own religious traditions have opposed. To imagine different religions working together musically blurs their incompatibilities, and requires downplaying the submission to religious authority that strong religions demand. Religion involves claims to truth, and the truths of different religions, in many cases, are mutually exclusive. The more these strong claims to truth and the conflicts among them decline in importance, the less authority religion carries. Thus adherents of strong religion have a point when they reject religious pluralism, seeing it as a watering down of religion that compromises faith and relativizes truth. John MacArthur, pastor of Grace Community Church in Sun Valley California, put the matter very succinctly in an interview with Larry King: "There is only one true and living God, and that's the God of the scripture. The God and Father of our Lord, Jesus Christ. And if you aren't praying to that God, you are praying to no one" (King 2003).

The relativizing of religion that conservatives complain about is not the only shortcoming of religious pluralism. The underside of celebrating pluralism is eagerness to make light of religion's violent aspects. Pluralists may want to tame religious violence through civility, and can cite many examples of neighbors making efforts to respect each other despite conflicting religious values. But the emotional forces that religion can rouse are not so easily civilized, especially in stressful situations. To tout religion as the common currency that citizens in a democracy share, and as the basis of their exchange and cooperation with one another, is to invite religious conflict and lend unwitting support to religion's capacity to inflame passion and escalate violence. Because of its capacity for deep emotional resonance, openness to multiple meanings, and special appeal to charismatic individuals, bullies, and demagogues, religion does not provide stable ground for either democracy or civility. While civil democracy requires freedom of religion, the reverse does not hold. Religion does not require civil democracy and may often threaten it.

The partisan political character of American public life exacerbates religion's tendency to incivility. From the bitterly contested election of Thomas Jefferson in 1800 to the political battles of our own day, public expressions of religion have often lined up in opposing political camps. The rise of the "religious right" in the 1980s fed on earlier battles against progressivism in religion and society, and the religious fundamentalism of the early 20th century had important antecedents in the debates over the Bible's stance on slavery that fueled the Civil War. Religious partisans have often wanted to suppress if not exterminate their enemies and make their own approach, be it pluralistic or old time religion, the basis of American democracy.

Liberal efforts to tie democracy and civility to religious pluralism feed the anxiety of conservatives who know ground has shifted away from older conceptions of religious authority and who resist the relativism of liberal progress toward pluralism. Both sides perpetuate a mythology about religion's role in American life; its hold on people's imaginations needs to be scrutinized and better understood. Rather than enlisting in one side or the other of the partisan war over which approach to religion should prevail, the time has come to agree that the ground has shifted and better understand the emotional and political forces working within that shift and resistance to it.

References

American Mercury (Hartford). March 17, quotations from 3.

Aurora. 1798. "For the Aurora, Friend Bache." Philadelphia, August 13, 3.

Burleigh [pseud.]. 1800. Editorial. *Connecticut Courant* (Hartford), July 7.

Eck, Diana L. 2001. *A New Religious America: How a "Christian Country" Has Become the World's Most Religiously Diverse Nation*. San Francisco: HarperCollins.

Jefferson, Thomas [1782] 1972. *Notes on the State of Virginia*. Edited by William Peden. New York: Norton.

King, Larry. 2003. "Religious Pluralism—Panel of Christians Speaks." *CNN's Larry King Live*, March 11. Television. Transcript available at allaboutreligion.org/religious-pluralism.htm.

Madison, James. [1785] 2003. *A Memorial and Remonstrance to the Honourable the General Assembly of the Commonwealth of Virginia*. Reprinted in *Church and State in American History: Key Documents, Decisions, and Commentary from the Past Three Centuries*, 3rd ed. Edited by John F. Wilson and Donald L. Drakeman, 63-68. Boulder, CO: Westview Press.

Pocock, J.G.A. 2003. *The Machiavellian Moment: Florentine Political Thought and the Atlantic Republican Tradition*. Princeton, NJ: Princeton University Press.

Sehat, David. 2011. *The Myth of American Religious Freedom*. New York: Oxford University Press, 60-67.

Slauter, Eric. 2009. *The State as a Work of Art: The Cultural Origins of the Constitution*. Chicago: University of Chicago Press.

Washington, George. 1939. *The Writings of George Washington from the Original Manuscript Sources: 1745-1799*. Edited by John C. Fitzpatrick. Vol. 30: June 20, 1788–January 21, 1790. Washington, DC: U.S. Government Printing Office. Accessed from George Washington Resources, University of Virginia Library, etext.virginia.edu/washington/Fitzpatrick.

Witte, John, Jr., and Joel A. Nichols 2011. *Religion and the American Constitutional Experiment*, 3rd. ed. Boulder, CO: Westview Press.

Civility, Religion, and American Democracy: Some Cautionary Reflections

Paul Boyer, University of Wisconsin-Madison

||||||||||||||||||||||||||||||||||||||||||||||||||||||||||||||||||||||||||||||||||||||||||||||||||||||||||||||||||||||||||||||||||||

Surveying the full span of United States history, has religion furthered or impeded civility? Obviously this is not an either/or question, but a rhetorical jumping-off point for discussion and reflection. In this essay, I focus mainly on Protestantism in America, and my understanding of "civility" in this context does not refer primarily to good manners or respectful personal relations among individuals or politicians, but rather to the root meaning of the word civility: structural relationships, broadly upheld by the constituent members of a given polity, that help create the requisite conditions of a civil society. In the American context, these conditions have historically included equal justice before the law, a democratic form of government, tolerance of diverse views and beliefs, and a general equality of condition.

Ample historical evidence exists to argue both sides of my opening question. In the antebellum era, Quakers and evangelical Protestants played leading roles in the antislavery movement, aimed at eradicating a glaringly uncivil social institution. Harriet Beecher Stowe, author of the abolitionist bestseller *Uncle Tom's Cabin*, was the daughter of one evangelical preacher, Lyman Beecher, and brother of four others, most notably Henry Ward Beecher. The abolitionist lecturer and editor Theodore Dwight Weld, a leader of the movement, was a staunch evangelical and follower of the famed evangelist Charles G. Finney.

During the so-called Progressive Era of the late 19th and early 20th centuries, liberal Social Gospel ministers like Washington Gladden and Walter Rauschenbusch applied their religious faith to the realities of urban-industrial America, with its sweatshops, dangerous factories, immigrant slums, and vast disparities of wealth and poverty—conditions radically inimical to a civil society. The British journalist William T. Stead appealed explicitly to Christian sentiments in his 1894 manifesto *If Christ Came to Chicago*, exposing the appalling conditions in that great Midwestern metropolis. Jane Addams, founder of Chicago's famed Hull House social settlement, clearly saw her commitment to serving the city's immigrant masses as an expression of her Christian faith. In terms of popular readership, the most influential book of the Social Gospel era was *In His Steps* (1896) by Charles M. Sheldon, a Congregationalist minister in Topeka, Kansas. (The influence of *In His Steps* continues to the present. The rhetorical question that Sheldon adopted as his subtitle, "What Would Jesus Do?", pervades the culture, including "WWJD" bracelets, charms, neckties, rings, key chains, and even teddy bears.)

In the 1950s and 1960s, religious leaders of all stripes, black and white, Protestant, Catholic, and Jewish, lent moral authority to the civil rights movement and the broader black freedom struggle to break the corrosive influence of racism on American civil society. The movement's leading organization in the early years was the Rev. Martin Luther King Jr.'s Southern Christian Leadership Conference (SCLC). The Rev. James Reeb, a Unitarian/Universalist minister and a member of King's SCLC, was bludgeoned to death in Selma, Alabama, in 1965, where he had gone to protest racial segregation. The National Council of Churches (NCC), an association of liberal Protestant denominations, lobbied and organized marches and letter-writing campaigns to promote the cause. In the months preceding passage of the landmark Civil Rights Act of 1964, the NCC held daily prayer services at a church near the Capitol to support the bill.

In short, religiously motivated individuals and groups, including many drawn from the ranks of Protestant Christianity, loom large in America's social-reform history. And this, in turn, is crucial to the preservation of a civil society and to overcoming the racial, ethnic, and class barriers that always threaten to fragment the commons into hostile, mutually distrustful enclaves.

But of course there's a darker side as well. Throughout American history, religious bodies and individual believers have also upheld uncivil institutions and fomented social discord. While many northern religious leaders and lay members embraced antislavery, many others abhorred the abolitionist cause. The owners of New England textile mills dependent on slave-produced cotton were often pillars of their local Congregational or Episcopal churches. Southern Protestants, meanwhile, cited selected biblical passages—from the story of Noah's sons to the letters of St. Paul—to justify slavery and a racial caste system. The Presbyterian, Methodist, and Baptist churches all split over slavery (among other issues) in the antebellum era, creating divisions that have long persisted. America's largest Protestant denomination, the Southern Baptist Convention, traces its origins to that long-ago division over slavery.

Protestant–Catholic hostilities have fostered incivility as well. In 1834, a Protestant mob burned down an Ursuline convent near Boston. Two years later, a group of enterprising Protestants in New York City published Maria Monk's *Awful Disclosures*, a sensational anti-Catholic polemic by an alleged ex-nun describing the lurid goings-on of priests and nuns in a Montreal convent, including the strangling of newborn infants whose bodies were tossed into a pit in the convent basement. This pamphlet and its purported author were soon exposed as frauds, but its malevolent influence lived on. Protestant anti-Catholic sentiment intensified in the later 1840s and 1850s as thousands of Catholic immigrants arrived from Germany and Irish Catholics flooded in, escaping their homeland's devastating potato famine. The anti-Catholic, anti-immigrant American (or "Know Nothing") party, which enjoyed a short-lived efflorescence in the mid-1850s, attracted many Protestant voters in Boston, New York, Philadelphia, Baltimore, and beyond.

The same years that gave rise to the Social Gospel and the industrial and municipal reforms of the Progressive Era also saw the emergence of a powerful moral-control movement especially targeting big-city immigrants—a movement with deep roots in Protestant America. The religious (and gender) origins of Frances Willard's Woman's Christian Temperance Union (1874) were manifest in its very name. The Anti-Saloon League (1893), a major force in the passage of the Eighteenth Amendment (Prohibition) in 1919, was led at the local and regional levels by hundreds of Methodist, Baptist, Congregationalist, and other Protestant ministers. Until its repeal in 1933, national Prohibition played a notoriously divisive role in American society and politics.

In the 1920s, some Protestants donned the white robes of the Ku Klux Klan, with its racist, nativist calls for white, native-born Protestants to rally in support of "One Hundred Percent Americanism." Indeed, the Klan's primary symbol was the Christian cross. In my home town, Dayton, Ohio, KKK crosses blazed in the night sky to intimidate students at the University of Dayton, a Catholic school operated by the Society of Mary. In 1923 my grandfather, pastor of a small evangelical city mission in Dayton, sadly expelled his Sunday school superintendent for joining the Klan.

In short, from a historical perspective, the role of religion in American civil society defies easy summarization. By carefully selecting one's evidence, one can build a plausible case that religious leaders, church bodies, and devout members of the laity have, indeed, at decisive moments in the nation's past courageously challenged entrenched forces diametrically opposed to a truly civil social order. In the words of a 1955 manifesto by the American Friends Service Committee, religious bodies and individuals, in the quest for a more civil society, have often stood ready to "Speak Truth to Power." Yet, sadly, the historical record also reveals many instances when religion's moral and social authority has buttressed and exacerbated the forces of conflict and incivility.

If the historical record is mixed, what of the present? By almost any measure, the United States is far more religious than any other industrialized nation, so considerations of religion are crucial to any discussion of civility in contemporary public life. Here, again, however, simple conclusions prove elusive. With new ideological alignments and cultural configurations, the more overt expressions of Christian anti-Semitism and of Protestant anti-Catholicism have faded—though neither has disappeared. Many religious groups, from national bodies to local congregations, continue to play notable roles in efforts to create a more civil society, and to create bonds across the barriers of race, ethnicity, religion, sexual orientation, and social class. Within Protestantism, the liberal mainstream denominations, the National Council of Churches, the American Friends Service Committee, the Unitarian-Universalist Association, and many other groups have spearheaded such efforts. In March 2011, an ecumenical alliance of Protestant, Catholic, and Jewish religious leaders mobilized to protest the hearings conducted by Representative Peter King, a New York Republican, to investigate radicalization among American Muslims—hearings widely criticized as an incitement to Islamophobia.

Among evangelicals, a few organizations, notably Jim Wallis's Sojourners movement and Ronald Sider's Evangelicals for Social Action, persistently raise issues of social justice and seek to promote civil discourse. Rick Warren, the Southern Baptist pastor of California's Saddleback Church, one of the largest and best-known of the independent megachurches that have proliferated since 1970, has stirred controversy among evangelicals for his efforts to promote peace and environmental protection and to combat poverty and disease—social-justice causes historically championed by more theologically liberal churches. Although standing firm against abortion rights, gay marriage, and the theory of evolution, Warren's positions on other issues are not those typically associated with conservative Protestantism. During the 2008 presidential campaign, Warren sponsored a "Civil Forum on the Presidency" at his Saddleback Church to "restore civility in our civic discourse." His invitation to Barack Obama to speak at this event unsettled many conservative evangelicals strongly opposed to Obama's candidacy.

But, as in the past, the picture is mixed. Contemporary U.S. Protestantism's kaleidoscopic diversity also includes a subset of evangelicals of a particularly fundamentalist cast whose role in the "civility" debate is considerably more problematic. Historically, the so-called "Fundamentalist" movement arose in the early 20th century amidst evangelical dismay over Darwin's theory of evolution and "modernist" tendencies among liberal church leaders and theologians, including the critical study of the Bible and Judeo-Christian history by paleographers, literary scholars, and archeologists. The defenders of imperiled orthodoxy insisted on the Bible as the inerrant Word of God and on the literal veracity of such doctrines as Jesus' virgin birth, resurrection, ascension into heaven, and Second Coming—doctrines the modernizers interpreted metaphorically or subjected to skeptical textual scrutiny.

Today's evangelicals at the fundamentalist end of the spectrum discern an absolute chasm dividing all humanity.[1] On one side are the saved, or "born again"—men and women who have accepted Jesus Christ as their personal savior and will live eternally with Christ in heaven. Outside this charmed circle of the redeemed are the unsaved, or "lost"—men and women who have rejected (or not yet heard) the Gospel message, and are thus doomed to eternal punishment. This cosmic bifurcation between saved and unsaved transcends race, ethnicity, social class, and political ideology—the categories typically viewed as the major impediments to a civil society and to respectful discourse in the public square.

When we move from the sphere of personal relationships to the public arena, the fundamentalist mindset comes into play even more decisively, shaping the believer's outlook on a wide range of social, political, and cultural issues. If one's position on such issues is seen as determining one's salvation and eternal destiny, then they are not open to debate or compromise. Finding common ground is not the point. These matters represent surface manifestations of an absolute division in the spiritual order, ordained by God and set forth in inerrant Scripture.

But perhaps countervailing influences are at play. In their impressively documented book *American Grace: How Religion Divides and Unites Us* (2010), Robert Putnam and David Campbell cite recent trends likely to reduce religion's divisive power: many younger Americans are abandoning religion altogether; tolerance of religious diversity, homosexuality, gay marriage, and premarital sex is growing; inter-religious marriages are on the rise; and most religious believers have neighbors, work associates, and even family members of a different faith whom they nevertheless like and respect. With the knack for phrasemaking Putnam first displayed in his 2000 book *Bowling Alone: The Collapse and Revival of American Community*, Putnam and Campbell call this the "Aunt Susan" phenomenon. Most Americans, they suggest, have among their relatives an "Aunt Susan" of a different religious persuasion.

These data and arguments merit serious attention. When applied to American society as a whole, all these trends doubtless are moderating the socially divisive effects of religious differences. But I suspect this is far less true for the subset of evangelicals that is the focus of this essay. The "Aunt Susan" effect may be less efficacious among those who hold their beliefs most tenaciously and/or who live in semi-hermetic social worlds in which their closest interactions are largely confined to others who share their religious dogmas. A Wisconsin public-school teacher recently told me of her sister and brother-in-law, fundamentalist believers, convinced that the Second Coming is near, who homeschool their children, attend a church of like-minded believers, and tolerate only reading matter and TV and radio programming that reinforce their worldview. When a daughter of the family recently asked her aunt, my informant, "Is it true that some people don't celebrate Christmas?" and the aunt replied, "Yes that's true. Jewish people celebrate a holiday called Hanukkah," the girl's mother angrily intervened and warned, "Don't talk to her about false religions!" Continuing for a moment in the anecdotal vein, I can report that a close boyhood friend has broken off all communication because he sees me as a traitor to the fundamentalist faith of our youth. I have cousins with whom I can enjoy friendly conversations on neutral topics or childhood memories, but beyond a certain point I am fully aware that I am viewed not only as a family member linked by ties of blood and memory, but also as someone on the other side of the cosmic divide—an object of loving concern, a subject of prayer, someone to be restored to the fold, if at all possible, before it is too late.

The growth of secularism and religious tolerance documented by Putnam and Campbell, on the one hand, and the intensifying religious fundamentalism that is also strikingly evident in contemporary American life, on the other hand, are, in fact, symbiotically linked and mutually reinforcing. While those in the former camp view fundamentalism as the hard, unforgiving face of a religious intolerance they wish to escape, the fundamentalists view the secularizing and liberalizing trends as further evidence of the absolute religious and moral polarization that their theological position teaches them to view as the intrinsic nature of human society and indeed of all reality.

Some of my own recent work has focused on the powerful role of Bible-prophecy belief in shaping and reinforcing this fundamentalist worldview (Boyer 1992, 1999a, 1999b, 2005). The sacred texts of all three Abrahamic religions are notoriously open to varied interpretations, and this is certainly true of the Christian Bible, incorporating as it does the Hebrew scriptures, or Old Testament. Some Christians find the Bible's core message in the Golden

Rule and the Beatitudes, the sayings of Jesus preserved in the Sermon on the Mount, and other passages that laud peace and justice, portray God as a tender shepherd, and valorize love for the poor, the stranger, the outcast, and even one's enemies as the highest good.

Others, however, find a quite different message. Carefully assembling selected passages from the Book of Revelation and other parts of the Bible, like the pieces of a picture puzzle, they discover an apocalyptic worldview that divides all reality into opposing forces of righteousness and evil, with righteousness ultimately triumphant and all wickedness annihilated. For millions of prophecy believers, this is not simply a reassuring affirmation that good will ultimately overcome evil, but a literal scenario of the Last Days, foretelling Christ's return as a god of war with the redeemed saints—an avenging army that will defeat the Antichrist (called "the Beast" in Revelation) and slaughter the Antichrist's millions of doomed followers at the Battle of Armageddon. After this cataclysmic denouement will come the Millennium, Christ's thousand-year earthly reign of peace and justice foretold in Revelation, chapters 20 and 21.

Prophecy preachers and popularizers elaborate highly detailed narratives of these end-time events, and identify specific "signs of the times," drawn from contemporary trends and current headlines, that both point to and lay the groundwork for the rapidly approaching finale. Whatever the details, the eschatological drama is invariably cast in black-and-white apocalyptic terms, with groups, institutions, nations, and world figures arrayed on a polarized cosmic grid, like iron filings exposed to a magnetic field. This view of sacred history has obvious real-world implications. From this perspective, for example, an Israeli–Palestinian peace settlement involving a two-state solution, shared governance of Jerusalem, and Israeli withdrawal from the West Bank, as advocated by the U.S. government, directly challenges God's plan for the region as revealed in the Bible, in which the land of the Jews will expand to the Euphrates River (Genesis 15:18) and a rebuilt Temple in a transfigured New Jerusalem will be the site of Christ's millennial reign.

Closer to home, prophecy believers tend to approach the divisive issues that have intensified partisan conflict, fueled the culture wars, and coarsened civic discourse not as questions to be debated in a spirit of amity and conciliation, but as matters of cosmic urgency, as humanity hurtles toward its final crisis. Atheism, agnosticism, gay rights, "secular humanism," evolutionary theory, the role of religion in the public sphere, America's status as a "Christian nation," even the extent of federal power and U.S. support for the UN and other global organizations—all fall into place as playing a role in the unfolding last-days scenario. These are not issues to be resolved through majority rule or reasoned debate. They are signs, clues to the End Times, laden with eschatological meaning.

The 9/11 attacks, paradoxically, were interpreted by many prophecy believers as evidence both of satanic forces already at work in the world, and—as Jerry Falwell and Pat Robertson famously insisted—of God's judgment on a once-righteous nation corrupted by unbelievers, pornography defenders, school-prayer opponents, radical feminists, and abortion-rights advocates. Long before 9/11, but more insistently thereafter, many prophecy expositors linked Islam to the rise of the Antichrist. One prophecy writer called it "a religion conceived in the pit of Hell" (Evans 2003). As a quick scan of the Internet makes abundantly clear, many also see Barack Obama as preparing the way for the Antichrist, if not the Evil One himself. Ecumenical movements and advocates of inter-religious dialogue are suspect, too, as forerunners of Antichrist's demonic world religion; computers, credit cards, and communications satellites are suspect as the technologies Antichrist will use to establish his brief but nightmarish global dictatorship.

Many Americans understandably dismiss such notions as ludicrous—best left to Jon Stewart, Stephen Colbert, the *Onion*, and the *Skeptical Inquirer*. Nevertheless, however one views it, this belief system has implications for issues of civility and the nature of our public discourse, since it is so resistant to compromise or debate. One can abandon it altogether, but so long as one remains within its orbit, little room exists for maneuver. From the apocalyptic perspective, the spiritual forces underlying all history are shaped by unbridgeable polarities. The very call for "civility" is itself suspect, blurring as it does the black-and-white clarity of the eschatological scenario. The eternal warfare between good and evil will end not through compromise, but when one side is defeated and the other victorious, as foretold in the apocalyptic scriptures.

Of course, the apocalyptic believer I have described is, in part, an ideal type, as the sociologist Max Weber used the term. Few men and women outside mental institutions are totally in the grip of this interpretive schema in its purest form, to the exclusion of all other considerations or moderating influences. And one must again emphasize that Protestant fundamentalism, reinforced by literalistic prophecy belief, comprises only one segment of the American religious mosaic.

But a significant segment of the population, continually reinforced by local pastors, televangelists, radio, internet websites, and prophecy magazines and conferences, embrace this vision of how the world works and how it will end. Mass-market paperbacks play a key role as well. Hal Lindsey's slangy prophecy popularization *The Late Great Planet Earth* (1970), exploiting Cold War fears of Russia and of nuclear war, was the nonfiction bestseller of the entire decade of the 1970s. The *Left Behind* series of prophecy novels by Tim LaHaye and Jerry Jenkins, launched in 1995, has sold over 70 million copies worldwide and a spawned a host of spin-off products, including a movie, video game, children's version, and dramatization aired on many Christian radio stations.

Opinion polls consistently find that, with varying degrees of intensity, a substantial minority of Americans embrace the apocalyptic worldview I have sketched. A carefully constructed 1996 survey of U.S. and Canadian religious attitudes found that 42 percent of the Americans polled agreed with the proposition, "The world will end in a battle in Armageddon between Jesus and the Antichrist" (Angus Reid Group).[2] More recently, the Pew Research Center, on the basis of a 2006 poll, reported that 35 percent of Americans view the Bible (including, of course, the apocalyptic passages) as the literal word of God (Masci and Smith 2006). Though such beliefs surface more frequently in the South and among those with a high-school education or less, they are strong in all regions and at all educational levels. (In the Pew poll, 19 percent of college graduates affirmed their belief in the Bible's supernatural origins and literal inerrancy.)

Despite many predictions that modernity and secularization would proceed in tandem, Protestant fundamentalism remains a powerful force in contemporary America (and in parts of the world reached by evangelical missionaries, televangelists, and mass-market books available in translation). If anything, the communications revolution associated with modernity has amplified and broadened the reach of fundamentalist beliefs and apocalyptic end-time scenarios. These beliefs are pervasive in major conservative Protestant denominations, including the gigantic Southern Baptist Convention, which claims more than 16 million members. They are widely embraced, too, in the burgeoning charismatic churches, Bible fellowships, and megachurches with their thousands of members that flourish outside America's traditional denominational framework. Jehovah's Witnesses and Seventh-day Adventists, with millions of members in the United States and worldwide, espouse their own distinctive end-time doctrines.

The absolutist morality and apocalyptic anticipations that characterize this sector of conservative evangelical Protestantism shape the civic discourse not only through the worldview that individual believers bring to the public sphere and the voting booth, but through the lobbying efforts of such groups as the Family Research Council founded by James Dobson; Donald Wildmon's American Family Association; Louis Sheldon's Traditional Values Coalition; John Hagee's Christians United for Israel; Tim LaHaye's shadowy Council on National Policy; Beverly LaHaye's Concerned Women for America; the Southern Baptist Convention's Ethics and Religious Liberty Commission, headed by the influential Washington lobbyist and frequent media commentator Richard D. Land; and a vast network of similar groups. In a recent *Wall Street Journal* op-ed piece, Richard Land (2011) warned against any retreat in the culture wars. For the Republican Party to compromise on the bedrock issues espoused by the Religious Right, Land declared, "would amount to political suicide." Recent polling by the Pew organization, Land insisted, proved that some 22 percent of Americans stood with him in firmly embracing "the conservative Christian movement."

I don't wish to overstate the pervasiveness or influence of these beliefs. Nor do I want to strike an unrelievedly negative note in this exploration of religion's role in the quest for greater civility in American public life. But I would conclude by reiterating a basic point: any serious discussion of religion in contemporary culture and politics must take into account the millions of citizens who bring to the public sphere an unwavering allegiance to religious dogmas that trump all other considerations, and an apocalyptic vision of human history as a divinely ordained drama that is rushing inexorably toward its final climax.

Notes

1. I use the term "fundamentalist" not to describe membership in a specific organization or religious body, but more generally to characterize those who embrace with special tenacity the beliefs summed up here.
2. Of this total, 28 percent "strongly agreed" with the statement, while 14 percent "moderately agreed." My thanks to Professor Mark Noll of the University of Notre Dame for alerting me to this poll, conducted by the Vancouver-based Angus Reid Group, a leading polling organization.

References

American Friends Service Committee. 1955. *Speak Truth to Power*. Philadelphia, PA: American Friends Service Committee.

Angus Reid Group. 1996. Canada/U.S. Religion and Politics Cross-Border Survey. Printout of survey results, October 11, 1996.

Boyer, Paul. 1992. *When Time Shall Be No More: Prophecy Belief in Modern American Culture*. Cambridge: Harvard University Press

_____. 1999a. "The Apocalyptic in the Twentieth Century." In *Fearful Hope: Approaching the New Millennium*, edited by Christopher Kleinhenz and Fannie J. LeMoine, 149-169. Madison: University of Wisconsin Press.

_____. 1999b. "The Growth of Fundamentalist Apocalyptic in the United States." In *Apocalypticism in the Modern Period and the Contemporary Age*. Vol. 3 of *The Encyclopedia of Apocalypticism*, edited by Stephen J. Stein, 140-178. New York: Continuum.

_____. 2005. "Biblical Prophecy and Foreign Policy." In *Quoting God: How Media Shape Ideas about Religion and Culture*, edited by Claire H. Badaracco, 107-122. Waco: Baylor University Press.

Evans, Michael D. 2003. *Beyond Iraq: The Next Move—Ancient Prophecy and Modern Day Conspiracy Collide*. Lakeland, FL: White Stone Books.

LaHaye, Tim, and Jerry Jenkins. 1995-2007. *Left Behind* series. Wheaton, IL: Tyndale House Publishers.

Land, Richard. 2011. "Americans Don't Want a 'Truce' on Social Issues." *Wall Street Journal*, March 4. online.wsj.com/article/SB10001424052748703300904576178390519502436.html.

Lindsey, Hal. 1970. *The Late Great Planet Earth*. Grand Rapids, MI: Zondervan.

Masci, David, and Gregory A. Smith. 2006. "God is Alive and Well in America." *Pew Forum on Religion and Public Life*, April 4. pewresearch.org/pubs/15/god-is-alive-and-well-in-america.

Monk, Maria. 1836. *Awful Disclosures*. New York.

Putnam, Robert D. 2000. *Bowling Alone: The Collapse and Revival of American Community*. New York: Simon and Shuster.

Putnam, Robert D., and David Campbell. 2010. *American Grace: How Religion Divides and Unites Us*. New York: Simon and Shuster.

Sheldon, Charles M. 1896. "In His Steps." *The Chicago Advance*.

Stead, William T. 1894. *If Christ Came to Chicago! A Plea for the Union of All Who Love In the Service of All Who Suffer*. Chicago: Laid & Lee.

Religious Pluralism and Civility

Wade Clark Roof, University of California, Santa Barbara

IIIIIIIIIIIIIIIIIIIIIIIIIIIIIIIIIIIIIIIIIIIIIIIIIIIIIIIIIIIIIIIIIIIIIIIIIIIIIIIIIIIIIIIIIIIIIIIIIIIIIIIIIIIIIIIIIIIIIIIIIIIIIIIIIIIIIIII

In their new book, *American Grace: How Religion Divides and Unites Us* (2010), authors Robert D. Putnam and David E. Campbell argue that religion in the United States divides us in what we believe and how we practice faith, the traditions we honor, and in the political ideologies with which we are associated. Yet at the same time, Americans interact with people of different faiths at work, in friendships and social networks, and increasingly in marriages and families, all of which expose us to differing views about God and faith and serve as a check of sorts on the possibility of serious divisions. For sure, the United States has not experienced the depths of religious tensions and conflict as have many other parts of the world, and no doubt this is due in great part to our nation's democratic religious context.

And yet, despite its obvious truth, Putnam and Campbell's argument comes across as a bit glossy. American history has had its serious moments of incivility, even violence—anti-Catholicism, anti-Semitism, anti-Mormonism, lynchings, bombings of abortion clinics, and more recently tensions with, and at times overt hostility toward, Muslims on the part particularly of conservative Christians. Worries about radical Muslims within the United States have escalated in the years since the events of September 11, 2001. Eurocentric religious roots run deep within our culture, often deeper than we care to admit, and are associated with all sorts of "evils" as we now define them, such as racism and gender discrimination. And the potential for religious-based incivility on still another scale is intensified, living as we now do in a global world where the "religious other" is brought more clearly into our everyday presence. When violence breaks out elsewhere in the world, inevitably there are repercussions here. The events in the Middle East during the so-called 'Arab Spring' produced tensions and demonstrations among Arab-Americans in our own cities. The point is that in a diverse and global religious context, civility in its most elementary sense—respect among people—becomes very fragile, easily strained by broader social, political, and economic conditions around the world. Religion itself is enmeshed within its social and cultural environment, so much so that we often lose sight of the religious amidst all else that is a part of that complex whole, or alternatively, the social, political and economic realities may themselves take on the appearance of being religiously based when we actually cannot reduce social reality to a single dimension. However we perceive the religious in relation to these other contextual realities, we must begin with the assumption that social reality is itself a complex phenomenon.

I suggest that the issue of civility and religion is complex and deserves far more attention than it typically receives. But first, a clarification: religious diversity and religious pluralism are hardly the same. Diversity refers to the fact that many religions may co-exist with one another, whereas pluralism has to do with the quality of the relations among such groups. Diversity is a given, it simply is, but pluralism is what we make of that diversity—how we define it, what we do with it. Hence pluralism might be properly thought of as a culture: it exists to the extent it is socially cultivated and maintained, widely appreciated, and welcomed as a human ideal—if, perhaps most importantly of all, it is genuinely practiced.

Now, to turn to civility and religion. My comments are framed around three interrelated points about how these two are connected and appear to be changing in our time. As we shall see, connections among the two are deeper than surface impressions might suggest, and hence we need to explore carefully what is involved if indeed the nexus between the two is shifting.

First, as the early French sociologist Emile Durkheim would remind us, when addressing civility we must take seriously the character of a nation's social solidarity, or what it is that holds it together. The values and practices of civility are linked and indeed reflect that solidarity. Of course, much of the glue that holds the United States together is capitalism and consumption, popular culture, and utilitarian individualism. So powerful are these cultural and economic forces that we confront a problem if we think that religion as conventionally described is what really unites the country. In an earlier time, we could have said that a core Protestant culture was a strong unifying force, and Christianity of course remains influential, but in the contemporary, incredibly diverse religious context, one that includes a growing non-affiliated religious sector, any argument about national unity as based upon shared religious beliefs and practices is obviously stretched. Public conversation about religion has become increasingly divisive, often requiring clarification as to what religion are we talking about, to what extent beliefs and ethical values can be generalized, and how are we to deal with deep religious differences. Religious diversity within a society, as Peter Berger likes to point out (1967), erodes certainty and shared definitions of social reality.

Not surprisingly, traditional religionists, and particularly conservative Christians, yearn for a return to a time—largely mythical—when the moral and religious foundations of the country were presumed to be more widely Christian, if not evangelically Christian. And others—Jews, Muslims, other minorities, many moderate-minded Protestants and Catholics, and secularists—argue instead that the nation's foundations lie not in any narrowly defined faith tradition but in what Barbara A. McGraw (2003) calls the nation's "sacred ground." By this she refers to the broadly conceived normative framework that governs all religious belief and practice in the United States—that is, laws and customs such as the separation of church and state, voluntary faith, the sacred quality of conscience, equality, and freedom of religion or no religion—as stated in, or inspired by, the First Amendment to the Constitution. Describing the American religious system, McGraw observes that:

> its theological principles are grounded, not in a conception of a divine order to be reflected in the social order, but in the individual and her relationship to God. Consequently, to the degree that coercive power was granted by the founders to government authorities, its objective is theological—to protect and preserve God's relationship with individuals and the expressions of conscience that derive from it, but not to determine what conscience should direct. (17)

So the two perspectives can be distinguished as follows: the first emphasizes a particular substantive set of beliefs and values, notably Christian, as a basis of national order, the second the shared principles of the individual rights of Americans in matters of faith and practice. For lack of better labels, we might describe the two constituencies holding these perspectives as traditionalists versus progressives, particularly in the way they define core American values. Both of their voices today are loud with respect to how they view the presence of religion within the public arena. We hear appeals to the foundational principles behind both voices, with religious and cultural traditionalists distinctly at odds with progressive, more liberal Americans about how best to think of the country in relation to religious authority, and implicitly how this basis of authority relates to our understanding of civility. The split between the two is at times tense and probably has increased in intensity over the past quarter century. Religious communities themselves are internally divided between exclusivists who believe that their faith is uniquely true and those with more inclusive views, believing that all religions have some truth and wisdom. This internal split appears to be growing in the large mainline faith communities. A Pew survey in 2007, for example, shows that upwards of 70-80 percent of Americans in these communities now believe there are many paths to salvation, and thus are at odds with the 20-30 percent who continue to hold to more narrow, exclusivist views. This split is just the opposite within the more conservative communities where exclusivist views clearly dominate.

More is involved here than simply a view of salvation. Research shows that traditionalists are also more likely to hold authoritarian, judgmental images of God whereas progressives favor images that are more nurturing and supportive, a split that also appears to have increased (Froese and Bader 2010). Of course, there are corresponding differences in the myths Americans hold about their God and country. Those holding to authoritarian images of deity, and believing that there is only one way to salvation, are more likely to espouse notions of American goodness and innocence, and that the United States holds God's chosen people and is the millennial nation charged with carrying democracy and true faith to the rest of the world (Hughes 2003). Thus the differences in thinking about salvation are not just religious in some narrow sense of personal faith but affect a much broader, encompassing worldview—with regard to notions about God in relation to the country and the world.

When thinking of God in relation to the country, the issue of social solidarity arises: to what extent and in what way does religion contribute to the bonding of Americans as a nation? Helpful here is a distinction that philosopher Charles Taylor makes in his recent volume, *A Secular Age* (2007). He distinguishes between "neo-Durkheimian" and "post-Durkheimian" types of social solidarity. Fundamentalist and other conservative religious people are neo-Durkheimians in the sense of trying to hold on to, if not restore, an older order that was more monolithic religiously and thought of as a widely shared faith; they appeal to an authoritarian God and to the notion of a Christian nation. On the other hand, progressive-minded religious Americans across the major faith communities, along with minority religious populations and the non-religious, are post-Durheimians because they appeal to the rules, principles, and procedures embedded in law and practice governing how religion should operate in a democratic order. In effect, national solidarity in a diverse society like the contemporary United States cannot rest on the substance of any one particular faith, even that of the historically dominant faith tradition, but rather increasingly upon the "sacred ground"—prescribing freedom of individual religious choice and conviction for all Americans. The implications for civility are obvious: only in the latter case where the nation-state is defined independently of a particular religion is civility understood to arise out of a common humanity that it is rooted in fundamental human values. Anything less amounts to tolerance by the chosen religious group of all others, itself hardly a sufficient foundation for civility in an increasingly large and religiously diverse society.

This conflict over foundational principles today is framed largely as political ideology, most evident in partisan politics and thus very visible in the public arena. Religion and politics are particularly aligned in our time, and has been so since the Reagan years of the 1980s. But in 2004, it became apparent that attendance at religious worship services was the best predictor of voting Republican in the presidential election; this pattern remained evident in the 2008 election but was weaker. But there is something more here than simply an overlap of institutional affiliations. Sociologist James Davison Hunter (2010) is correct, I think, when he argues that "public life" is now thoroughly politicized, that is, it has come to be largely reduced to the political. Put differently, political action is now the primary means whereby religious influence in American society occurs. Partisan voting, support, and mobilizing of individuals and groups have become, so to speak, religious acts, both for the right and the left, each adhering to what might be thought of as a "political theology." This conflation of the religious and the political implies, as Hunter goes on to write, that "the politicization of everything is an indirect measure of the loss of a common culture and, in turn, the competition among factions to dominate others on their own terms" (107). Note the gravity of his terms: the situation today is one in which there is the loss of a broadly unifying culture in relation to politics, and consequentially, intense competition, or contestation among factions, to dominate and control the social order, and thereby bring about change in keeping with the faction's own distinctive theological vision of a good society.

Particularly important is how this plays out religiously in the struggles between traditionalists and progressives. Both draw selectively off religious teachings, symbols, and narratives to construct their own political theology and related strategies of political action, and often with a degree of intensity not unlike that of missionary zeal. That these political theologies greatly differ—addressing similar issues but from opposite ends of the ideological spectrum—testifies to Hunter's point about the deep politicization of our culture. Yet despite radical differences, they share a theological hermeneutic of trying to garner influence through the power of political rhetoric—be it that of electoral politics or as found in the language of non-governmental organizations. These latter organizations are of great importance in this respect: they mobilize supporters through mass mailings and the Internet and advance one or another cause by means of conflating religious, moral, and political symbols. That is, they "politicize" religion and morality and, conversely, "religionize" and "moralize" politics, thereby creating generalized ideologies that are at once powerful and compelling. With both partisan politics and the NGOs, the venue for bringing about social and political change is largely the state and its structures, be it through appeal to its laws, policies, and procedures, or by means of enacting new legislation and/or overturning older court decisions. Consequently, so-called religious concerns whether of the left or the right are forced into a rather similar, structurally determined format which can be dealt with, or is complicit with a Constantinian alliance of religion and the state. Civility is extended to others, or limited to them, in what amounts typically to the use of political weaponry as a means of expressing religious conviction and action.

There is also the politicization of ritual, particularly what we call civil religious ritual. Recall George W. Bush's and Barack Obama's presidential inaugurations. At the first Bush inauguration in 2000, the ceremony closed with a benediction given by the president's Methodist pastor from Texas saying that his was a "humble prayer in the name that's above all names, Jesus the Christ. Let all who agree say, Amen." To the contrary, Obama's inaugural address testified to the nation's diversity: "For we know that our patchwork heritage is a strength, not a weakness. We are a nation of Christians and Muslims, Jews and Hindus—and nonbelievers." His was a plea for a unity based not on Christianity, not on any particular religion, but on the basis of a common humanity. This contrast in ritual aptly illustrates Taylor's distinction between the two types of social solidarity—the "neo-Durkheimian" affirming a religious-based solidarity and the "post-Durkheimian" with its affirmation of a normative framework respecting diversity and the freedom of individual choice. Obviously as these two recent inaugural ceremonies indicate, we are living in a time when the very core of our national identity as expressed through civil religious rhetoric is hotly debated.

Finally, and implicit in the argument about the importance of the normative religious framework, civility rests less upon consensus in belief than upon respect for people's differing views. Given all that I have said about political theologies and the differing types of social solidarity, it should be obvious that there are limits to achieving consensus in a society like our own. More important—and far more critical to civility—is the willingness to engage the other, to listen, and to respect those with whom you disagree. Civility in a democratic order implies a degree of openness to the other, the recognition that society exists as an ongoing exchange of ideas and views between us—inevitably an affirmation of our coexistence. Civil debate involves trying to understand better where the other is coming from, and indirectly, where we are coming from when we disagree with one another. We must ask not just how our visions of a good society differ, but also why, and how they can be enhanced through conversation. In the practice of civility, might we even come to recognize that our own views are better understood even by ourselves—perhaps actually enriched—through dialogue? Again a quote from Charles Taylor is helpful:

> People can also bond not in spite of but because of difference. They can sense, that is, that the difference enriches each party, that their lives are narrower and less full alone than in association with each other. In this sense, difference defines a complementarity. (2002, 191)

Thus I conclude with a reminder of what Tocqueville observed almost 175 years ago, that civility rests upon deeply embedded cultural "habits" that sustain respect for, and dialogue with, those with whom we disagree. Since Tocqueville's time the country has faced many challenges calling for the extension and application of such habits—be it in addressing racial and ethnic differences, gender, or more recently gay, lesbian, bisexual, and transgendered populations. Each time we have addressed one another over the course of our history, we have in a very real way discovered something anew about the richness and beauty of the human. And now very much on our minds is the challenge of religious diversity including how the religious and the nonreligious themselves can bond together. Perhaps in exploring this latter complementarity we will learn even more about the depth of our human condition as Americans.

References

Berger, Peter L. 1967. *The Sacred Canopy: Elements of a Sociological Theory of Religion.* New York: Anchor Books.

Froese, Paul, and Christopher Bader. 2010. *America's Four Gods: What We Say About God—and What That Says About Us.* Oxford: Oxford University Press.

Hughes, Richard T. 2003. *Myths Americans Live By.* Urbana: University of Illinois Press.

Hunter, James Davison. 2010. *To Change the World: The Irony, Tragedy, and Possibility of Christianity in the Late Modern World.* New York: Oxford University Press.

McGraw, Barbara A. 2003. *Rediscovering America's Sacred Ground: Public Religion and Pursuit of the Good in a Pluralistic America.* Albany: State University of New York Press.

Pew Forum. 2007. United States Religious Landscape Survey. religions.pewforum.org.

Putnam, Robert D., and David E. Campbell. 2010. *American Grace: How Religion Divides and Unites Us.* New York: Simon and Schuster.

Taylor, Charles. 2002. "Democracy, Inclusive and Exclusive." In *Meaning and Modernity: Religion, Polity, and Self,* edited by Richard Madsen, William M. Sullivan, Ann Swidler, and Steven M. Tipton, 181-194. Berkeley: University of California Press.

_____. 2007. *A Secular Age.* Cambridge: Harvard University Press.

III
Architecture

Architecture and Civility

Ayad Rahmani, Washington State University

|||||||||||||||||||||||||||||||||||||||||||||||||||||||||||||||||||||||||||||||||||||||||||||||||||||||||||||||||||||||||||||||||||||||||||||||||||||||||||||||||||||||||||||||||||||||||||||||||||

As Joan Ockman says in her essay, "democracy in architecture…is never self evident or stable." She even describes the connection as metaphoric, suggesting that democracy is at least once removed from the central concerns of architecture. Indeed architecture neither speaks nor acts politically but simply rises with brick and stone to accommodate function and give shelter. It certainly does not get up and yell "you lie" as Joe Wilson now famously did to rebut the president in the middle of his speech.

Or so the conventional thinking goes. Yes, architecture is mute, but that does not mean it is without impact on democracy and civility. In fact I argue that it is central to the making of democracy. It provides space for people to gather and realize their collective voice as was so recently and amply demonstrated in Tahrir Square in Cairo, Egypt, and others like it across the Middle East. The Arab Spring, the phrase given to the recent uprisings in the region, would not have happened without it.

This does not necessarily bode well for our context here in the United States, a country overrun by suburbs and where private property and individualism remain marks of the national identity. Even with gas prices bordering on $4 a gallon, the majority of Americans still favor the suburbs over living in the center of the city. A few exceptions stand out, most notably New York City and Portland, Oregon, two cities that have done a tremendous job instituting policies and building infrastructure to empower their citizens to live close, consume less, and, ultimately for us here, connect with each other and the world around them democratically. Can a society speak of itself as a democracy when a good part of its members don't know each other and largely communicate only through the airwaves? This is a serious question that this country will have to ask itself as it moves into the future.

In his essay, Alan Plattus speaks of architecture and democracy in slightly different terms. Beyond the setting itself, he sees architecture as providing the occasion for citizenship, by which he means architecture is a field of practice that opens before the public an opportunity to form community and engage in civil discourse. He sees the potential for architecture to generate the kind of ameliorative discourse that can turn adversarial positions into positive ones. As a form of public art and a spatial one at that, architecture is inherently inclusive of diverse interests and can serve the aims of more than one group. Bringing two or three opposing groups to talk about a public intervention such as a park, library, or homeless shelter could easily help these groups find mutual goals and ultimately discover again the simple but often forgotten truth that we are all here seeking happiness and stability. Very few of us are inherently bent on hell and, more often than not, when reacting negatively are simply doing so to defend a cause, territory, or name that we may feel is at risk of slipping into obsolescence.

One could only imagine what would happen if, rather than being separated by a debilitating wall, the Palestinians and the Israelis were to talk about a common bridge, literally or metaphorically—a school or a public market that both can share and grow from. Architecture for Plattus is unique in this sense; it helps those in contention sidestep their political differences, only to return to them objectively through a constructive narrative based on mutual benefits and shared beliefs.

If the link between architecture and democracy may require some rhetoric to construct, that between architecture and civility is easier to imagine. It can be built on a more literal ground. A building can demonstrate civility or incivility by the way it, in the words of Witold Rybczynski, either "respects its surroundings" or "call undue attention to itself." A civil building is also one that "implies a sense of decorum or propriety." Interestingly, both Rybczynski and Ockman credit Mies van der Rohe, one of the pioneers of modern architecture, for being a very civil architect even though, at the face of it, he designed buildings that stood out from their surrounds. According to Rybczynski, despite Mies's significant contribution to modern architecture, he was at heart "an Edwardian" whose buildings exhibited a high degree of "sober propriety." Nowhere is this more the case than in the Seagram Building in New York, an intervention so proper it steps back in a gesture of old respect to a building across the street and one well recognized by history and the architectural community: the McKim, Mead and White 1916 beaux arts New York Racquet Club.

Ockman contrasts Mies, a midcentury modernist, with Koolhaas, a post-industrialist. Neither architect wants to be "merely civil" for this could easily degenerate into lies and cynicism. There is nothing worse than agreeing with a client simply to be agreeable when in fact the work that is being produced is unattractive, dysfunctional, or just downright mundane. But where Mies trod gently, Koolhaas moved in brashly. His "vortex-like" library calls attention mainly to itself, but in so doing, also to the city's architectural "vacuity." How did Koolhaas sell his bold slap in the face to the city and the public to which the library is meant to serve? That might indeed be Koolhaas's genius, working as a magician bandying one product with one hand but in reality pushing another with the other. Here Ockman cleverly distinguishes between "public accountability" and "public relations management" and says that "despite the unusual lengths to which the library's representatives went to invite local input and to keep Seattle's citizens informed," it is difficult to decipher whether Koolhaas's intentions were to achieve the first or the second—accountability or management.

Whether we are aware of it or not architecture impacts the way we think of ourselves and our societies. Buildings and settings are an expression of our collective will and care; the meaner looking they are the more likely they are to generate in us a commensurate feeling of worthlessness and neglect. No one would want to believe in democracy if the place to which that democracy belongs does not reflect shared values. This is Ed Feiner's main thesis. In his role as the chief architect leading the design excellence program of the General Services Administration department of the U.S. government, he sought to steer the way toward a more holistic approach to the role that architecture can play in public life. Public buildings can be narrowly viewed as the product of function and taxpayers' money, but they can also be valued as buildings that reflect the "creativity, inventiveness, strength, and diversity of the American people." They can encourage dialogue between the people and their government. Perhaps this is where democracy and civility should begin.

Shared Difference:
Citizenship and Civility in
American Architecture and Urbanism

Alan J. Plattus, Yale University

|||||||||||||||||||||||||||||||||||||||||||||||||||||||||||||||||||||||||||||||||||||||||||||||||||||||||||||||||||||||||||||||

If a distinguishing and celebrated characteristic of the American concept of citizenship is the assumption of the autonomy of the individual citizen as a basis for any larger idea of collective identity or responsibility, then surely American architecture is entitled to a similar starting point. And yet that very assumption, of the autonomy and freedom of the individual building relative to the collective ensemble of the street, square, neighborhood, or city, is often taken to be the root cause of a deep-seated and pernicious incivility in American architecture and urbanism. At least since the late nineteenth century, the rationale for architecture and the emergent field of city planning have been couched in terms of the need to "civilize" the visually chaotic, and therefore morally suspect, cities produced willy-nilly by laissez-faire development patterns composed of unregulated and uncoordinated individual decisions, presumably motivated principally by self-interest rather than any larger idea of the common good. And while there has been a recent communitarian critique of the extreme versions of individual freedom that have produced hypertrophic manifestations of individualism in contemporary consumer culture, and at the same time have apparently stymied collective action and shared responsibility in an age of single issue politics, this is nothing like the consistent condemnation of stylistic and typological individualism in architecture by critics both domestic and foreign.

But much of that critique misses a crucial distinction: between an urban landscape of recognizably autonomous buildings that are, at the same time, articulate parts of a larger formation in which each must play a role, and a landscape of formally and/or functionally microcosmic buildings and larger projects, in which each part stakes a claim to be a self-sufficient enclave. The latter world may, in fact, be beautifully designed and planned to create the appearance of a high level of coordination and even civility, but insofar as individual buildings and building complexes pretend to have no need to communicate, collaborate, or connect, they ultimately create a landscape of potentially enormous real incivility: exemplified, perhaps, by the gated communities in the United States (and now, increasingly, around the world), especially when those communities are themselves composed of miniaturized suburban representations of the legitimately autonomous rural villas of a traditional agrarian and aristocratic society. But autonomy, of either buildings or citizens, does not imply an absence of mutual dependence that encourages a degree—often a high degree—of civil interaction, often across an apparently wide divide of significant difference.

I would, therefore, like to argue that a characteristically American urbanism based on the relative autonomy of individual buildings and other urban elements that then enter, like citizens, into relationships, contracts, conversations, and debates based on mutually agreed upon rules and conventions, can not only create spaces of considerable—if idiosyncratic and tenuous—civility, but can also recognize, accommodate, and represent a degree of individuality and difference that is necessary for a meaningful public realm, not to mention a contemporary concept of citizenship, in a way that more traditional models of both citizenship and urbanism grounded in authority and obedience cannot. What one might call the Hobbesian view of architecture—that left to their own devices, individual architects, their clients, and the buildings they produce will never give us a coherent and civilized public realm—certainly has plenty of highly publicized evidence to support it, but also a great deal of less celebrated counter-evidence in the form of ordinary commercial and residential streets in countless towns and cities, town greens and courthouse squares, streets and corridors, and even industrial infrastructure and landscapes, much of which was produced before zoning codes and other explicit design controls. Not only do these urban, suburban, and rural landscapes have a pattern, an order, and even a beauty of their own that observers such as J.B. Jackson and Robert Venturi have tried to teach us to appreciate, they also have openness and resilience that the more controlled, composed, and apparently "orderly" urban landscapes do not possess.

Let's take a couple of examples. The New Haven Green is one of the oldest planned public spaces in North America: planned, but unlike its European precedents and contemporaries, only in two dimensions. Its ambitious scale—almost four times as large as the fully enclosed and three-dimensionally designed Place des Vosges in Paris—meant that for most of its early history the loose collection of buildings around its perimeter struggled to provide a frame for this evolving civic space. Appropriately, as the city flexed its civic muscles, it was the space itself, and some of the buildings in it, that were first designed as a coherent whole, enclosed by a fence and landscaped by monumental elm trees, remaining relatively autonomous from the far more casual development of the urban fabric on its four sides. Indeed, each of those sides was shaped according to quite distinct patterns of use: commercial to south, civic and financial to the east, residential and eventually civic to the north, and monolithically institutional to the west. The latter, a product of Yale's Old Brick Row plan of 1792, had been wonderfully open to the Green up to the 1870s, when it was replaced by the fortified quadrangle of the Old Campus. However, the remainder of the sides consisted of individual buildings, each of which established its own relationship to the street and beyond to the Green, and to its neighbors. What they shared was rarely a style, a size or scale, or even a typology, but rather an address. If anything, for much of their history, the buildings around the Green probably exhibited rather greater variation in their manners and appearance than the citizens passing by.

By the late 19th and early 20th century, however, the ethnic and cultural diversity of New Haven's population, like that of so many American industrial cities, quickly caught up and probably surpassed the heterogeneity and presumptive chaos of the built environment, even provoking a bit of a reaction. In New Haven, that took a variety of forms, including the monolithic Gothic wall erected by Yale College facing the Green, but also the slightly later Colonial Revival architecture of many public as well as commercial buildings, recalling nostalgically a (partially fictionalized) era of greater urban homogeneity, if not civility. But in the late 20th and early 21st century, the Green has become (again?) what Yale sociologist Elijah Anderson (2011) has called a "cosmopolitan canopy" in the heart of a city still undergoing dramatic and often wrenching change. The return of a diverse urban, and even regional, population to the hearts of beleaguered American cities like New Haven is a complicated story, in part of gentrification, but also of the process Anderson identifies as the temporary suspension of suspicion and fear grounded in difference within the more or less demilitarized (if still policed) zone provided by urban spaces such as Philadelphia's Reading Terminal. In such spaces, Anderson argues, difference is neither abandoned nor obliterated, but rather recognized and tolerated, often at a level still not fully embraced by urban designers and their clients who may create those spaces willy-nilly.

Of course the terms of the possible creation or discovery of new and/or revitalized cosmopolitan canopies is precisely the issue for architecture and urbanism. Do we only inherit or discover spaces of mutual recognition and shared identity by good fortune, or can such spaces be shaped, seeded, or even created by a process of conscious and/or collective design? The unavoidable fact is that our faculties of criticism have been rather better cultivated in recent years than our ability to suspend disbelief long enough to work toward, or at least recognize, the positive opportunities of a constructively engaged public realm. We know and have rehearsed all the reasons why urban space might be unavailable for a genuinely civic experience: its increasing privatization, the reduction of public life to spectacle, the repressive policing and surveillance of public space, etc. One of the refreshing aspects of Anderson's exploration is the implicit suggestion that it might be possible, and even quite useful, to bracket those concerns and attend to what actually goes on, both socially and architecturally, in a particular space, relative to other spaces within a city, while maintaining a realistic and tough-minded critical stance with respect to the larger context. From this perspective, the opportunities afforded an architect might turn out to be less the grand and iconic gesture, and more the role of joining, and hopefully adding to, a conversation already in progress. One can see this sort of process at work in the streets of a medieval city like Bologna, where stylistically and economically autonomous structures share both an underlying typology and a commitment to contribute to the collective space of the street through the shared conventions of façade making and the arcade, but one can see a version of it as well in the main streets and courthouse squares of Texas towns, giving the lie to the all too familiar assumption that the only choice available for American urbanism is the radical, even anarchic, independence of the individual building or the master planned and coded ensemble of urban designers. It is certainly worth considering, especially in an American context, that future cosmopolitan canopies may turn out to be the public sum of a variety of private parts, created through the typically messy democratic process of negotiation and plain old horse trading.

Now this is not at all what the ambitious founders of American urban design and the urban planning profession had in mind when, with an eye toward the achievements of European urbanism in the second half of the 19th century, they proposed what they clearly considered necessarily dramatic antidotes to the environmental and social degradation of the cities produced by laissez faire industrial capitalism. A central premise of this movement, whether represented by the grand plans and monumental architecture of the City Beautiful, or the progressive urban reforms of the "city practical," was to temper individual entrepreneurial energy (greed) with a sense of collective responsibility (urban design). At its best, this impulse introduced organizing structures of enormous power and public good—parks and park systems, public institutions and buildings—into the admittedly raw and problematic fabric of American cities and urban life. However, at the other end of an apparently unavoidable continuum, progressive reform phased over into paternalism and even repression. And when they ran against, rather than with, the spatial and political grain of the American city, plans like those of the City Beautiful movement condemned themselves to irrelevance, or at least a frustrating, but probably characteristic and quite interesting, tendency to partial realization over time as fragments that ironically re-enter the discourse of the city as autonomous episodes in their own right. This is part of what Thomas Bender (2002) has identified in his recent discussion of New York as the "Unfinished City," but it may well be typical, allowing of course for considerable and equally characteristic local difference, of most American cities.

Even Washington, D.C., for all its pretensions to a unified grand plan supported by a coordinated entourage of monumental architecture, will never be mistaken for Versailles or St. Petersburg. It is, like the government it houses, another characteristically American product of a myriad of individual development and design decisions and a host of competing and partially realized plans, not the clear and consistent outcome of a founding document continuously guiding its faithful followers. That is not to say, especially in the somewhat peculiar case of Washington, that these decisions were not made with awareness and even reference to the founding documents and their ongoing interpretation, but rather that the interpretive process was and remains open and pragmatic, even fraught and contested, in a way rarely seen in older European capital cities, where the controversial exceptions are just that, as opposed to American urbanism (or for that matter politics) where each new case is potentially exceptional. When that more open and unpredictable process of give and take has been abrogated, as with the endless process of design control and review that has been the case in Washington for some time, and is now being exported in the form of tightly regulated design codes to communities that seek to protect their "character," not to mention their property values, the product is not so much civility as it is homogeneity, and even boredom. Thus the mind and eye-numbing homogeneity of the least-common-denominator architecture and urbanism of much of Washington development in the 1980s, surpassed only by the chillingly civil architecture on both sides of the Wall in post-war Berlin. And if one form of urban civility borders on the authoritarian and the other, equally authoritative, might be best described as corporate, the cumulative result with respect to urban life and space seems disappointingly similar.

Nor is the artificial simulation of visual and programmatic diversity much better. Festival marketplaces and "lively" urban redevelopment projects like Times Square are, in terms of process and the resulting version of the public realm, not all that different from master planned communities and frozen-in-(fictitious) time preservation projects like Williamsburg. They are perhaps best diagnosed by what they exclude: spontaneity, unpredictability, genuine difference of taste and culture, and most of all the productive tension and occasional conflict from which cities draw their energy and capacity for change and invention. These characteristics are not in fact obliterated alto-gether, any more than what planners like to call "conflicting uses." Rather they are relegated to marginal positions along with the populations they serve and represent, creating a city not of constructive civic interaction which actually tests and extends the capacity of civility, but rather an all-too-familiar city of fortified enclaves and widening, and increasingly unbridgeable, gulfs, only mitigated by the occasional cosmopolitan canopy, where difference may be more represented than engaged.

My suggestion is that from the point of view of architecture at least, the entire city should be seen as a cosmopolitan canopy, sheltering a diversity of buildings, uses, and users not otherwise to be found in such proximity and concentration. Great public spaces such as Main Streets in American cities in particular cut a revealing slice through this diversity, rather than mobilizing a stage set of imposed uniformity or, for that matter, simulated diversity, to mask it. In that respect, the American city is, as has occasionally been pointed out, more like Serlio's Comic stage set, although even his Tragic set exhibits considerably more *varietas* than many theorists and critics would attribute or allow in classical urban design. It is possible, in this context, to see the American gridiron plan itself as a kind of urbanistic cosmopolitan canopy: exploiting and even celebrating the irony that the planning template of greatest homogeneity—and therefore detested by the designers of the City Beautiful movement—can sponsor the highest level of architectural autonomy and diversity. This is in part a historical rather than theoretical phenomenon, as in the case of the New Haven Green and the famous nine-square plan of which it is part, as the build-out of an ambitious founding plan has proceeded over long periods of time, and usually through private development of individual parcels, with minimal or purely local reference to the plan as a whole. And yet within that apparently unplanned (or post-plan) process, the plan itself, what Aldo Rossi (1982) would have identified as an urban artifact, not only holds its identity as a framework, but even enforces a peculiar kind of civility and grudging mutual respect on the apparent cacophony of individual buildings and developments. Here again, the alternately horrified or exhilarated reaction of observers—mostly European it turns out, although they have powerfully influenced local practitioners who might have known better—who have seen the grid as the agent of either radical liberation or urbanistic damnation, turns out to be as simplistic as many outside reactions to the American version of democratic politics.

So if American urbanism, like much of American culture and politics, is inevitably constructed within a perpetual, and mostly productive, tension between individual autonomy and collective ideals and aspirations, what about the spaces within and through which we construct, enact, and celebrate a sense of common purpose and even community? Will they be, at best, cosmopolitan canopies, under the shelter of which difference is observed and tolerated, only to be unleashed again as intractable disagreement and even incivility once we return to our respective corners of the city: homes, schools, neighborhoods, and voting booths? Lacking all but a provisional and transitory version of the more stable and foundational idea of a "common vision," upon which a fully unified and monumentalized space of collective identity would be grounded, it might seem we are condemned to identify, and be identified, with an ever-changing landscape of mainly private development, within which exists a weak version of a public realm, often associated with buildings and images of a more or less distant past, or, perhaps at best, a romantic image of nature, fenced off for control and admission or grafted into the real world of ongoing urban life. And yet, not only can we return to the New Haven Green, or for that matter the ubiquitous courthouse squares of American Midwestern towns, to find what the historian of New Haven Green, Rollin Osterweis, characterized in 1976 as the almost perfect living symbol of the familiar, but urbanistically precise, slogan *e pluribus unum*, we can also now update that distinctive idea of a space of shared difference in terms of new public spaces like the High Line in New York City, not a space created from scratch as the center of a new city, but rather a rediscovered and recycled piece of old industrial infrastructure, becoming a splendid new cosmopolitan thread weaving together otherwise disjointed old and new buildings, views, and people. It may be that "civility" is no longer the appropriate term to describe the spatial relationships constructed by a new urban experience like the High Line, except insofar as it reminds us that there are no *a priori* rules, codes, or standards of taste for the design of a civilized city, only the conventions that are established, and sometimes provisionally codified, by shared patterns of development and use. American urbanism, at its best, demonstrates civility because it chooses to do so, not because it is required to. Civility in architecture, as in politics and daily life, is therefore more like what the architectural historian Vincent Scully has characterized as a conversation over time, than like an orchestra conducted by a maestro, and it is particularly the case in American civil society and urbanism that there must be space for new, even strange or strident voices to join the conversation without being shouted down in the name of an inappropriately or prematurely closed idea of citizenship or civility.

References

Anderson, Elijah. 2011. *The Cosmopolitan Canopy: Race and Civility in Everyday Life*. New York: Norton.

Bender, Thomas. 2002. *The Unfinished City: New York and the Metropolitan Idea*. New York: New Press.

Osterweiss, Rollin G. 1976. *The New Haven Green and the American Bicentennial*. Hamden, CT: Archon Books.

Rossi, Aldo. 1982. *The Architecture of the City*. Cambridge, MA: MIT Press.

Civility and Architectural Propriety

Witold Rybczynski, University of Pennsylvania

||||||||||||||||||||||||||||||||||||||||||||||||||||||||||||||||||||||||||||||||||||||||||||||||||||||||||||||||||||||||||||||||||||

The *Oxford English Dictionary* defines civility as "Behavior proper to the intercourse of civilized people; ordinary courtesy or politeness, as opposed to rudeness of behavior; decent respect, consideration." What does this mean in an architectural context? A civil building could be said to be one that respects its surroundings. In a city, for example, it takes its place on the street while observing the often unwritten code of the place, and it does not usurp its neighbors or call undue attention to itself. Similarly, in a rural setting, a civil building does not put on fancy airs, unless it is a very large country house, in which case a manicured lawn or *parterre* may mediate between the architecture and surrounding nature.

But architectural civility involves more than just fitting in—it also implies a sense of decorum or propriety; that is, an appropriate relationship between what a building contains and what it looks like. Long ago, the Renaissance architect Andrea Palladio observed of residences:

> One must describe as suitable a house which will be appropriate to the status of the person who will have to live in it and of which the parts will correspond to the whole and to each other. But above all the architect must observe that for great men and especially those in public office, houses with loggias and spacious ornate halls will be required, so that those waiting to greet the master of the house or to ask him for some help or a favor can spend their time pleasantly in such spaces; similarly, smaller buildings of lesser expense and ornament will be appropriate for men of lower status. (1998, 77)

Palladio's observation about "those in public office" suggests that not only should a house look like a house, whether it is more or less grand, but that a public building such as a courthouse should look like a courthouse. The converse is also true. When a residence resembles a public building, we say it is pretentious; on the other hand, when a public building lacks presence, it strikes us as mean and inadequate.

Unfortunately, there are many buildings today that do their best to stick out rather than fit in, and many courthouses that look too much like offices, just as there are many private offices that look like public buildings. This lack of civility has many causes. A coarse, publicity-oriented culture values buildings that call attention to themselves, no matter their function. The popular media places a premium on originality and is likely to give more coverage to an outrageous building than a demure one. Stephen Holl's eccentric Simmons Hall at MIT, for example, is a student dormitory that the architect himself described as inspired by a sponge; despite functional drawbacks, it was widely covered by the architectural press. William Rawn's exemplary but distinctly lower-key student residences at Northeastern University, across the Charles River, received less attention (although they garnered many architectural honors). The hurried nature of modern life privileges the architectural one-liner and the built equivalent of the sound bite over subtlety. And the entertainment ethic that affects all aspects of American life today, from politics to the arts, likewise imposes itself on architecture. When a well-known architect unveils a new building, the public has come to expect the architectural equivalent of a fireworks display.

What follows are several examples of how changes in our concept of civility have affected two very different kinds of architectural structures: skyscrapers and memorials.

Skyscrapers

Skyscrapers, which are so prominently visible in a city's skyline, have long acted as advertisements for their owners; this was certainly the case with the Woolworth Building in New York and the Chicago Tribune Building in Chicago. On the other hand, the Empire State Building, designed by Shreve, Lamb & Harmon in 1929-30, was not a corporate headquarters, which may be why its design is relatively low key. The style is an example of early American modernism, a blend of Beaux-Arts composition (Shreve and Lamb were both *anciens* élèves who apprenticed with the great Beaux-Arts firm, Carrère & Hastings) and a stripped, Art-Deco sensibility. While necessarily prominent, the Empire State Building exhibits admirable restraint, the result only partly of construction economics. Like most skyscraper designers of that period, Lamb reduced the building's mass with height and only allowed sculptural effects on the peak.

The RCA Building (30 Rock), the centerpiece of Rockefeller Center, is generally attributed to Raymond Hood, who famously beat Eliel Saarinen a decade earlier in the Chicago Tribune tower competition. Hood's prize-winning design was Gothic, but in the RCA he adopted Saarinen's abstract, picturesque massing and produced an evocative stalagmite that is still one of the best skyscrapers in Manhattan. Unlike Van Alen's flamboyant Chrysler

Building, RCA is perfectly deadpan, no jokes or ornamental flourishes; the art in the building is left to artists such as Lee Lawrie, Leo Friedlander, and José María Sert, whose work adorns the street level exterior and the lobby.

Ludwig Mies van der Rohe was civil to a fault. While he did not modify his designs to suit either their purpose—the steel-and-glass curtain wall he invented served equally for offices, apartments, and courthouses—he did adjust his designs to fit their surroundings, whether it was Park Avenue in the case of the Seagram Building, Lake Michigan in the case of the Lakeshore Drive apartments in Chicago, or a small-scale Montreal street in the case of Westmount Square. While a pioneer of modernism, Mies was in many ways an Edwardian, and his buildings, especially in the post-war period, exhibit a high degree of sober propriety. A later modernist, Eero Saarinen, who was a student of Hood at Yale, used black granite rather than bronze for the CBS Building, but his design exhibits an equally sober demeanor.

Renzo Piano's New York Times building exposes its structural bracing (which recalls Mies's unbuilt proposal for the Chicago convention center), but Piano's is otherwise an equally restrained design although favoring lightness and transparency. The vast newsroom is a special feature of the building's base, but the tower itself plays down that it is the home of a prominent newspaper, although it has a large billboard-like sign on Seventh Avenue, a commercial gesture that it is hard to imagine either Mies or Saarinen making.

The competition for the design of the New York Times building, won by Piano, included a proposal by Frank Gehry with Skidmore Owings & Merrill. Gehry's design, which also incorporated a giant *New York Times* logo, was unconstrained by convention, appearing to melt at its base and blossom at its peak. Such mannered architectural gestures are increasingly common in what are usually called "signature buildings." Like many uncivil acts, Gehry's achieves its impact by playing against common custom. Another iconoclastic design is the so-called Turning Torso, a residential tower in Malmö, Sweden, designed by Santiago Calatrava. There is little economic rationale for a 54-story skyscraper in a small city with no tall buildings, and even less for an apartment tower that twists. The spiral shape is intended to be a gateway marker visible from the new Öresund Bridge that links Denmark and Sweden, its putative iconic status apparently excusing any excess. The spiral concept reappears in Zaha Hadid's twisting tower, one of a trio planned for the Fiera Milano. Its neighbor, Daniel Libeskind's curvaceous skyscraper, looks like it is made of Jell-O. The Fiera is a trade fair, so perhaps a circuslike atmosphere was considered appropriate.

Memorials

Memorials are intended to stand out from their surroundings. However, they, too, have traditionally exhibited a high degree of propriety with respect to the person or event being commemorated. The Washington Monument was the tallest manmade structure in the world when it was built. Were this merely a memorial to the first president it could be accused of bombast, but it is also meant to be an urban landmark on the National Mall as well as a national symbol. Thanks largely to Thomas Lincoln Casey's simplification of Robert Mills's rather overwrought design, it has a pleasing abstraction that balances its enormous size. It also has a high degree of ambiguity, an essential attribute for a memorial. The giant obelisk includes no information about the first president, not even his name, allowing the viewer to privately form his or her own opinion.

The District of Columbia War Memorial, also on the Mall, commemorates the 499 citizens of the district who gave their lives in World War I. The *tempietto*, designed by Frederick H. Booke, belongs to an age that used a variety of commemorative conventions: pylons, urns, steles, and statues, adjusting the scale to fit the importance of the individual, group, or event. In fact, the little temple-like memorial is actually a bandstand, designed to accommodate the 80-member U.S. Marine Corps Band, which John Philip Sousa conducted in a concert on inauguration day in 1931.

Franklin D. Roosevelt once told his friend Supreme Court Justice Felix Frankfurter, that, in the event a monument was erected to his presidency, he wanted something no larger than his desk. To commemorate the 20th anniversary of Roosevelt's death, a group of his friends carried out his wish and placed a block of marble, approximately 7 feet long, 4 feet wide, and 3 feet tall, in front of the National Archives Building on Pennsylvania Avenue. The simple inscription was likewise Roosevelt's idea. What would he have thought of his later memorial (designed by Lawrence Halprin) that sprawls over 7.2 acres and includes numerous water features, statues, art works, walls, and copious inscriptions?

Halprin's design marks an important moment in the evolution of memorials, because it is the first "landscape" memorial on the Mall, occupying so much space, and attempting—not always successfully—to convey a wealth of information in words and images, a veritable commemorative theme park. Subsequent memorials have followed the example of the FDR Memorial, no longer *marking* a place, but *becoming* a place. The nature of these places is resolutely pedagogical and invariably incorporates a multitude of images, quotations, data, history, and associated educational aids. Even the Vietnam Veterans Memorial, which is as minimalist and ambiguous, in its own way, as the Washington Monument, spreads out over 3 acres. The Korean War Veterans Memorial occupies a similarly large area, and attempts, with little success, to incorporate a multitude of elements: a granite wall, images of GIs, statues of soldiers, copious written information, a reflecting pool, and a flagpole. The memorial finally sinks under the weight of all this information.

The centerpiece of the Martin Luther King Jr. memorial, beside the Tidal Basin, is a colossal statue of King 30 feet tall. This is the tallest statue on the Mall; by comparison, the statue of Jefferson in the memorial across the basin is 19 feet high, as is Daniel Chester French's seated Lincoln. Bigger has definitely become better in the world of memorial building. Such inflation of memory can be interpreted as a kind of incivility, since it turns commemoration into propaganda and a sort of marketing.

Conclusion

While incivility has long been a feature of American political life, as the recent evolution of skyscrapers and memorials demonstrates, architectural incivility is something relatively new. It is related, I believe, to the blurring of the distinction between what is public and what is private. "Proper" behavior in the public realm used to mean behavior that was different from what was acceptable at home: ladies wore gloves in public, gentlemen wore hats which they removed on entering a home. There were public places where "jacket and tie" was the rule; conversely, removing a jacket or loosening a tie indicated a social shift, as did "rolling up one's sleeves." There was always a line between what was public and what was private. Of course, the line was drawn slightly differently at different times and in different cultures; nevertheless, distinctly different norms of behavior, dress, and even speech prevailed in the home and in the street.

An architectural equivalent of this public/private divide is the sharp distinction that has always existed between a building's public exterior and its private interior. The exterior, likely to last a long time, is usually designed with a good deal of restraint compared to the interior, which might be altered over the years according to the whims of fashion. The exteriors of Baroque palaces, for example, tend to be dressed stone, monochrome and rather severe compared to the interior décor, which sports mirrors, colorful wall and ceiling paintings, and plenty of gilt ornament. How different is a building such as the new Cooper Union, designed by Thom Mayne, whose exterior is as equally whimsical and theatrical as its interior?

The modern age has, to a great extent, eradicated the line between public and private, or rather, in the name of individual freedom and informality—or perhaps simply laziness—the boundary of what was previously considered private behavior has been extended into the public realm. This is true in dress, speech, and comportment. The man's tie, long a symbol of public propriety, is in the process of disappearing—even President Obama feels comfortable appearing in public tieless (just as President Kennedy made history by appearing hatless at his inauguration). And costumes previously reserved for private activities—sweat suits, bathing suits, athletic gear, pajamas—have appeared on the street. Young people regularly sit or sprawl on the floor or ground in public places—a form of behavior previously restricted to beggars or the homeless. People, including politicians, cry at the drop of a hat. Intimate secrets of private lives are revealed on television talk-shows and on social media websites.

This easing of social norms may be seen to be either refreshing or discouraging, but it is relentless and irreversible. It also, not surprisingly, has had a profound effect on architecture, since the way we dress our buildings often mimics the way we dress ourselves. Many buildings today are the architectural equivalent of the backward-turned baseball cap: iconoclastic, fashionably irreverent, and—like headgear worn indoors—uncivil.

References

Palladio, Andrea. 1998. *The Four Books on Architecture*. Translated by Robert Tavernor and Richard Schofeld. Cambridge, MA: MIT Press.

On Democracy and Civility in American Architecture

Joan Ockman, University of Pennsylvania

For two centuries American architects have associated the forms of their buildings with ideas about democratic society. Beginning with Thomas Jefferson's Academical Village at the University of Virginia, efforts to create a democratic architecture have ranged widely from the "organic" philosophy of individual freedom and American exceptionalism of Louis Sullivan and Frank Lloyd Wright at the turn of the twentieth century, to modernist visions of a collective and egalitarian architecture in the 1920s and '30s, to the "new monumentality" after World War II, to the populism and pluralism of postmodernism. At times the rhetoric has been as notable for its hubris as for its idealism. During the early Cold War, for example, "architecture of democracy" became a slogan associated with the embassies and hotels that leading U.S. firms were triumphally exporting around the world as representations of the cultural values being vaunted in the name of the American Century.[1] More recently, democratic architecture has been bound up with a discourse of "public space"; the latter, in turn, has at times devolved into a set of minimum requirements for plazas and outdoor sculpture. Today "green architecture" risks becoming a similar kind of cliché, relying on bureaucratic regulations to quantify environmental appropriateness.

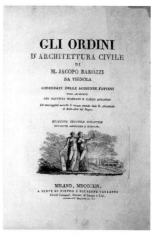

The word *civility* has found its way into architectural parlance less frequently in recent times, although the related idea of a civil or civic architecture goes back to the Renaissance, when it was codified in classical treatises as an area of building practice distinct from military architecture. In the early eighteenth century the Earl of Shaftesbury defined civility in terms of good breeding and "a right taste in life

Gli Ordini d'Architettura Civile by M. Jacopo Barozzi da Vignola, Milan, 1814.

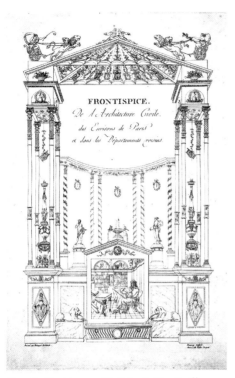

Recueil d'Architecture Civile by J. Ch. Krafft, Paris, 1812, frontispiece.

and manners," or refined social performance (Anthony [1737] 2001, 339.) Since then, civility in architecture has presumably signified a correspondence between architectural forms and social norms. As such, while connoting the qualities of urban and spatial decorum, the term also contains a sense of *decorousness*. While partaking of the political, it carries a nuance of *politesse*, or excessive politeness: implying an ethos of self-restraint and discipline, it seems to sanction docility or even effeteness. Compared to *democracy*, which retains a certain robustness, *civility* has a recessive ring.

My aim is not to split semantic hairs, and few people would argue for reducing architecture to good manners. But for the reasons just given it is worth being cautious about turning civility into a new architectural watchword. It is essential to bear in mind that architecture, whatever else it is, is an act of poetic imagination. If architecture reflects life, it does so—as Bertolt Brecht said of the theater—with special mirrors (Brecht 1964, 204). Its task is not only to fit in and accommodate, but also to raise questions and even, on occasion, to be obstreperous. The architect need not always say an unqualified yes to the client. As in the well-known cartoon by Saul Steinberg depicting two businessmen sitting across a desk smiling amicably at one another while a large thought balloon emanating from the one who is in charge reads "No," it is possible to register a *sotto voce* dissent in architecture by being subtle, tongue-in-cheek, or, indeed, arch. But frequently it is preferable to address things more frontally, and literally (in the case of buildings) to push the envelope. Take, for example, the "New Brutalism" in the 1950s, a deliberately tough, rough architecture strenuously defended by its inventors, the English architects Peter and Alison

Smithson, as "ethical" rather than "aesthetic."[2] Or to take another example, consider the shock administered by Robert Venturi, Denise Scott Brown, and Steven Izenour's 1972 book *Learning from Las Vegas*, which by scandalously celebrating the "ugly and ordinary" American landscape as an architectural virtue—or at least a pedagogical value—effectively reversed modernism's elitist pieties with respect to "high" and "low" forms of culture (Venturi, Brown, and Izenour 1978, 128 ff). Frank Gehry did something similar in his famous early house for himself in Los Angeles, made out of chain-link fence and other degraded materials, flying in the face of his conventional neighbors—and initially eliciting from them a not-in-my-backyard reaction—but changing the course of architecture. One could give many such examples from the history of architecture that had the result of renovating the discipline.

At the same time, the fact that architecture is an aesthetic and heavily mediated form of cultural production implies that the stakes with respect to the consequences of incivility are rarely as high as they are in a more direct arena of social practice like politics or religion. On the other hand, it is also clear that architecture has a profound capacity to affect human experience and relations through its spatial and material attributes. It can cheapen or ennoble; it can be inhospitable or welcoming; it can be deadening or exhilarating; it can be oppressive or liberating. It does not take a behavioral psychologist to observe that certain physical environments are more conducive to constructive forms of public encounter and interchange than others. As recent news demonstrates, democracy does not depend on real space for its enactment; citizenship tends to find places of representation and performance wherever it has to—not only in the rotunda of the Wisconsin State House and the pavements of Tahrir Square but also on the Internet. Yet however potent the new social and electronic media are proving themselves to be, citizenship practices continue to assume their most vivid expression in actual spaces. In this context, architecture can aid and abet its aspirations.

It has also been the case in recent years that architecture has aimed to be more than just a backdrop, increasingly striving to act as an experience or an event in its own right. The Italian architect Aldo Rossi once described the task of the architect as to set the table for the meal to take place (Rossi 1981, 5). But architecture now frequently wants to be the meal itself. And in today's media environment, the consumption of this sort of architecture has the capacity to have real effects. This was the case in the late 1990s, for example, with Gehry's Guggenheim Museum in Bilbao, which, by dramatically spurring tourism, caused a decaying and provincial city in the Basque region of Spain to be rejuvenated and transformed almost overnight. The "Bilbao effect" spawned many would-be Bilbaos in the subsequent decade (although more recently, with the bursting of the economic bubble, appetites and budgets for this particular urban strategy have diminished somewhat). But the implications of the recent crop of architectural spectacles for democratic discourse and civic life are at best equivocal. And as already suggested, the meaning or metaphor of democracy in architecture, or of civility, is not self-evident or stable.

From this perspective I would like to consider two emblematic works of architecture that illustrate some of these contradictions. Separated by almost half a century, they bracket what might be described as a shift in architectural practice and culture from the monument to the spectacle. The first example is the Seagram Building in New York, designed by Ludwig Mies van der Rohe. The second is the Seattle Public Library's Central Library, designed by Rem Koolhaas. Both these buildings refuse to be "merely" civil. And each radically reimagines and alters the rules of its urban context.

Completed in 1958 on Park Avenue in midtown Manhattan, the Seagram Building has famously been described as glacially "aloof" and imbued with a "tragic" self-awareness of its separation from the city (Tafuri and Dal Co 1979, 340). This description, by the Italian architectural theorist and historian Manfredo Tafuri, a critic of Marxian persuasion, was intended as praise. Sitting well back from the street on an elevated plinth, the thirty-eight-story building sublimely overlooks the urban scene from behind an austere bronze-colored glass-and-steel facade. By its refusal to engage with its surrounding context—in Tafuri's view—the building registers its distance and dissent from the capitalist

The Seagram Building.
Chicago History Museum, HB-29050, Hedrich-Blessing.

city. Tafuri quotes the Austrian writer Karl Kraus: "He who has something to say, step forward and be silent" (339).

Tafuri's reading is not entirely correct, in my opinion, and even a little melodramatic. Indeed, it is possible to view the Seagram Building as a paragon of urban decorum. Not only its classical symmetry but its setback from Park Avenue, painstakingly finessed along the sloping side streets, has the effect of relating it all the more directly to McKim, Mead and White's 1916 Beaux-Arts Racquet and Tennis Club across the street, with which its entry is exactly on axis. At a civilized distance, the high-modern Seagram thereby lends dignity to its neoclassical neighbor. While its granite plaza and laconic demeanor project a message of "do not enter" to those who have no business inside, its siting provides welcome relief from the incessant urban flows of traffic and pedestrians.

As far as Tafuri's capitalist critique is concerned, Mies hardly had any qualms about working for corporate clients (1970). Indeed, upon emigrating from Germany to the United States in the late 1930s, he quickly became one of their favorite architects, adding prestige and refinement to luxury apartment towers and office headquarters. The Seagram Building remains one of the most lavish buildings in New York, not Marx but rather Medici in its custom-designed mail chutes, fire alarms, and bathroom fittings (Lewis Mumford called it the "Rolls Royce" of contemporary buildings when it opened [1958, 19]). It is also interesting to compare it to its other iconic neighbor, Lever House, which was completed six years earlier by the firm of Skidmore, Owings & Merrill and stands diagonally across the street one block north. In an effort to palliate what was at the time a shocking disruption of the traditional street wall, Lever House has a three-story base that is built out to the edges of its corner site even as its slim shaft of office floors rises from just one-sixth of its footprint. This offers pedestrians access to its transparent lobby, which contains public exhibition space as well as elevators. It also accommodates the street-level amenity of a landscaped courtyard open to all. In the tower above, the bright and well-planned office floors provided the original employees—a largely female work force—with an unusually generous standard of workspace. Until the building's sale in the late 1990s, the paternalism of Lever Brothers' founder was duly noted on a plaque affixed to a stainless-steel-clad column at the entry to the courtyard.[3] Yet these benevolent urban gestures tend to get swept up in the slope and flux of the avenue, and the shiny blue-green curtain wall with its horizontal glass banding and flush metal frame lacks Seagram's elegantly articulated *gravitas*. If Lever House projects a more "democratic" image, Seagram exhibits the greater civility vis-à-vis the urban milieu. Yet both buildings, with their different deportments, contribute something of value to the urbanity of midtown Manhattan, and in ways not predetermined by their architects. On special occasions, Seagram's plaza is given over to curated public performances or the display of art; more regularly its edges are appropriated by denizens of the densely populated local office buildings as impromptu ledges for eating lunch.

We may also note that history is fickle with respect to the reception of buildings. While Lever House initially appeared a brash architectural gesture, within less than a decade it was replicated up and down the avenue by imitations of lesser quality (with the exception of the transcendent Seagram). And by the time the gargantuan Pan Am Building (now Met Life) was completed in 1963 ten blocks south at 45th Street, designed by Walter Gropius and his associate Pietro Belluschi, Lever House appeared practically demure. Straddling Park Avenue north of Grand Central Station, Pan Am closed off the view corridor like a big thumb in the city's eye (or, as the artist Claes Oldenburg travestied it, a melting Good Humor Bar [1965]). A cartoon in the *New Yorker* read, "It's a sad state of affairs when Lever House begins to seem like a warm old friend."[4]

Another fifteen years on, Rem Koolhaas would celebrate Manhattan's "culture of congestion" in his book *Delirious New York*. For the Dutch architect, monotony in the city is a far worse offense than incivility. Indeed, for Koolhaas, precisely what cities have to offer besides propinquity is cultural stimulation and the experience of difference. This urban philosophy would come to fruition in 2004 in his design for the Seattle Public Library. Unlike Seagram—the headquarters of a whiskey company whose owner made his fortune during Prohibition and thus desired to burnish his company's reputation with an exclusive, buttoned-down monument—Seattle was a deliberate effort by the city to create an urban "attraction," a building that would reverse the lackluster image of its downtown and, through the glamor and prestige of an internationally acclaimed architect, put Seattle on more than just the regional map. Traditionally an august temple of knowledge, the municipal library was now radically reprogrammed by Koolhaas as a building type for the 21st century. He based his design on both updated functional criteria—the obsolescence of books—and irreverent formal ones. As Ayad Rahmani noted in an article published in a Seattle design magazine just after the architect made his initial presentation of the project to the public, the scheme overturned all established hierarchies and brilliantly reconceptualized the library as a space of urban happening (Rahmani 2000, 24–26).

The Seattle Central Library.[5]

Was Koolhaas's gesture a democratizing one? Or was its radicality a slap in the face of Seattle's conservative public taste? The client was the most public possible, the city's central library system, and primary funding for the project came from a citizen-approved bond measure. The design process was exceptionally well-documented and was meant to be maximally public, as befitting the creation of an institution that should have, as the city librarian put it, the "transparency of democracy."[6] Yet despite the unusual lengths to which the library's representatives went to invite local input and to keep

Seattle's citizens informed about the project's development, and despite the architect's acquiescence to requests to make himself or his team available, it is difficult to say whether the process was more about public accountability or public relations management. As another early commentator pointed out in an essay titled "Just How Public Is the Seattle Public Library? Publicity, Posturing, and Politics in Public Design," written when the building was in its final stages of construction, the design ultimately incorporated a handful of suggestions that came out of the protracted community discussions but differed little in substance from the architect's original diagram (Mattern 2003, 15–17). This is not too surprising. Notwithstanding Koolhaas's vaunted design methodology ostentatiously based on "research," public opinion has never been among his privileged data sets.

As far as the building itself is concerned, its vortex-like presence in Seattle's downtown has undoubtedly pumped energy and excitement back into the heart of the city, much as Gehry's museum did in Bilbao. It has generated civic pride and boosted tourism. Unlike Seagram, though, Koolhaas's singular building does not try very hard to function as part of an urban ensemble; its hyperactive presence calls attention mainly to itself. From inside, the diamond-shaped grid of glass, cladding all exterior surfaces, deftly frames fractured vistas of the city. But they seem to accentuate the skyline's vacuity,

Overhead view of the main branch of the Seattle Central Library.[7]

and the carceral experience of looking out through the bars makes the library's occupants—in accord with the "paranoid-critical" method Koolhaas first elaborated in *Delirious New York* (1994, 235–36)—into voluntary or involuntary prisoners of architecture. While reviews in the press at the time the library opened were unanimous in declaring the building to be among Koolhaas's very best to date, and the continuing large crowds are prima facie evidence of its popularity, a number of observers have reserved final judgment. Among the latter, opinion seems to divide around whether one comes to the library primarily to enjoy its spatial and social performance, or to read books. From the second perspective, flaws in the basic circulation concept and shelving system as well as shoddy finishes have elicited a steady stream of complaints.[8] Perhaps in a project of this ambition and audacity such complaints are inevitable. But as a tourist who saw the building in 2006, what I found most remarkable was that the architect had managed to sell all that dazzling and extravagant glass to—of all people—librarians. Cubic volume not only takes precedence over bound volumes in the Seattle Public Library, but it also subordinates all other activities, however ingeniously and stylishly reconfigured, to the spectacle of architecture.

Thus from Seagram to Seattle. Whenever I try to imagine how a later period will look back at the architecture of this one, I think that the highly literal obsession with transparency and kinetics on the part of architects at the beginning of the 21st century—especially the fetish of escalators and ramps—will attest less to architecture's dynamism than to the profession's desperate attempt to compete with the warp speed of contemporary media and information. To approach architecture largely as a diagram of its circulation systems is a little like viewing the human body as an x-ray of the fluids moving through it.

Escalator in the Seattle Central Library.[9]

Still, the messenger cannot wholly be blamed for the message. A prominent public building like the Seattle Public Library is enmeshed in today's culture of spectacle, tied into an economy that demands a particular kind of renovation in order to attract global tourism, and designed for a client whose very raison d'être is threatened with extinction in the contemporary electronic maelstrom. Paradoxically, these social and cultural forces may be understood as having both democratizing and hollowing-out effects on embodied space. They are unlikely to promote civility. Yet architects can hardly deny these forces, even if it is also the task of their buildings to rise above them.

Notes

1. Statements by the hotel chain developer Conrad Hilton were typical: "Each of our hotels is a little America," designed "to show the countries most exposed to Communism the other side of the coin." See Hilton 1957, 327, 290; and, more generally, Wharton 2001.
2. On the New Brutalism, see Banham 1966.
3. The plaque read: "The mission of our company/ as William Hesketh Lever saw it/ is to make cleanliness commonplace/ to lessen work for women/ to foster health and/ contribute to personal attractiveness/ that life may be more enjoyable/ and rewarding for the people/ who use our products."
4. Cartoon by Weber 1963, 36.
5. Image is used under the terms of the GNU Free Documentation License, Version 1.2. Photo is by DVD R W and is available at en.wikipedia.org/wiki/File:Seattle_Central_Library,_Seattle,_Washington_-_20060418.jpg.
6. Cited in Mattern 2003, 5.
7. Image is used under the terms of the Creative Commons Attribution 2.0 Generic license. Photo is by Rex Sorgatz and is available at en.wikipedia.org/wiki/File: Seattle_library_main_branch_overhead.jpg.
8. On the building's flaws, see, for example, Cheek 2007.
9. Image is used under the terms of the GNU Free Documentation License, Version 1.2. Photo is by Robert Stein and is available at en.wikipedia.org/wiki/File:Library_esc2801.jpg.

References

Anthony [Ashley Cooper], Third Earl of Shaftesbury. (1737) 2001. *Characteristicks of Men, Manners, Opinions, Times,* vol. 1, *Advice, &c,* edited by Douglas den Uyl. Indianapolis: Liberty Fund.
Banham, Reyner. 1966. *The New Brutalism: Ethic or Aesthetic?* New York: Reinhold Publishing.
Brecht, Bertolt. 1964. "A Short Organum for the Theatre" In *Brecht on Theatre: The Development of an Aesthetic,* edited by John Willett. New York: Hill and Wang.
Cheek, Lawrence. 2007. "On Architecture: How the New Central Library Really Stacks Up." *Seattle Post-Intelligencer,* March 26. seattlepi.com/ae/article/On-Architecture-How-the-new-Central-Library-1232303.php.

96   *Civility and Democracy in America*

Hilton, Conrad. 1957. *Be My Guest.* Englewood Cliffs, NJ: Prentice Hall.
Koolhaas, Rem. 1978. *Delirious New York: A Retroactive Manifesto for Manhattan.* New York: Oxford University Press.
_____. 1994. *Delirious New York: A Retrospective Manifesto for Manhattan,* new ed. New York: Monacelli Press.
Mattern, Shannon. 2003. "Just How Public Is the Seattle Public Library? Publicity, Posturing, and Politics in Public Design." *Journal of Architectural Education* 57(1): 5-18.
Mumford, Lewis. 1958. "The Sky Line: The Lesson of the Master." *New Yorker,* September 13.
Oldenburg, Claes. 1965. *Proposed Colossal Monument for Park Avenue, N.Y.C.—Good Humor Bar.* Image accessed July 2012 at christies.com/lotfinderimages/d53155/d53155791.jpg.
Rossi, Aldo. 1981. *A Scientific Autobiography.* Cambridge, MA: MIT Press.
Rahmani, Ayad. 2000. "Library as Carnival: Reflections on Rem Koolhaas's New Proposal for Seattle's Public Library." *Arcade* 19(2): 24-26.
Tafuri, Manfredo. 1970. "Lavoro intellettuale e sviluppo capitalistico," *Contropiano* 2 no. 70: 241–281.
Tafuri, Manfredo, and Francesco Dal Co. 1979. *Modern Architecture.* New York: Harry N. Abrams.
Venturi, Robert, Denise Scott Brown, and Steven Izenour. 1972. *Learning from Las Vegas.* Cambridge, MA: MIT Press.
_____. 1978. *Learning from Las Vegas: The Forgotten Symbolism of Architectural Form,* rev. ed. Cambridge, MA: MIT Press.
Weber, Robert. 1963. *New Yorker,* March 23.
Wharton, Annabel Jane. 2001. *Building the Cold War: Hilton International Hotels and Modern Architecture.* Chicago: University of Chicago Press.

Public Buildings: Civility and Democracy

Edward A. Feiner, Perkins+Will Design

From the very beginning of our nation's history, the founding fathers recognized the importance of architecture and buildings to convey messages to the general population. In fact, Thomas Jefferson practiced architecture as a "calling" almost as important as politics. George Washington fancied himself an architect even if his work was mostly restricted to his Mount Vernon estate. The founding fathers recognized that in all past important civilizations, buildings were a chronicle of the art and technology of that society. Even the political and religious realities of their times were recorded in stone, brick, and mortar. When the United States declared itself a "real" nation with a real constitution (unheard of at the time), it was important to communicate that fact both within and outside of the highly ambiguous borders of the new nation. How could the United States establish its rights as a seafaring nation at a time when Great Britain, Spain, and France ruled the waves? How could America be taken seriously when it had just emerged from merely being a "disorderly colony," recently liberated from the strongest Empire on the earth? In fact, it was not expected by the major powers of the time that the young revolutionary nation with its strange and exotic concept of government would endure. How could a nation founded on western European culture, technology, and economics survive over 3,000 miles away from what was perceived at that time as a "civilization"?

By 1812, the very existence of the United States was seriously tested by the major powers of the time as American ships were hijacked and sailors were impressed by their captors. In the closing moments of the War of 1812, the British burned Washington, D.C., partially to drive home the point that destroying symbols of a nation or an institution of any kind was a good way to delegitimize its existence.

So what does all of this have to do with buildings and architecture? Prior to the War of 1812 and the destruction of Washington, D.C., the Congress of the United States authorized that a new capital city be located on the banks of the Potomac River between the sovereign states of Maryland and

Virginia. That in itself was a symbolic compromise. It placed America's capital city between the emerging mercantile/industrial culture of the north and the predominantly agricultural culture of the south. However, it also symbolized that this new model of governance would be housed in a new city, although far away at that time from major population centers, and would be based on the highest artistic, technological, and cultural achievements of western civilization. The choice of the aesthetic or design character would be fashioned on Greek and Roman principles of order, strength, and dignity, even if it was to emerge from a swamp at the edge of the American frontier. Although the founding fathers knew that Greek and Roman concepts of democracy were not fully consistent with the new American model, to the rest of the world these notions could convey a sense of maturity and power, that America had "arrived." In some ways the selection of a formalistic, neo-classical aesthetic was an odd choice for the new nation since it was a nation born of revolution and was the leading voice at the time for modernity (at least in politics).

The city design for Washington, D.C., was developed by French architect Pierre L'Enfant and often characterized as a French ideal of city planning, while also imitative of the master plan of Virginia's colonial capital, Williamsburg. Today when visited by Europeans and people from around the globe, Washington, D.C., is considered America's most continental looking city. By the time of the Civil War some European friends and distracters may have toyed with one more chance to disprove that the American experiment really worked, but the city of Washington and the nation endured.

The early days of the nation were very difficult at best, and civility perhaps had a slightly different meaning then. People were still dueling and political discourse was greatly animated. Oratory was passionate and volumetric, considering that there were no microphones with loudspeakers at the time. The extremes of political thought were great but somehow the new nation developed a Constitution, which, to this essayist, is the embodiment of civility in written words. However even then, as today, the backdrop for messages was almost as important as the message. The Williamsburg, Virginia, Capitol Building was as important to Patrick Henry at his time as Tiananmen Square was to the protesters in China in 1989.

Places, architecture, and buildings can provide an environment that either enhances a message or trivializes it. If the Constitution of the United States set a standard for decorum, structure, and civility in words, the architecture of its "temple" could provide the inspirational backdrop for its implementation. The original U.S. Capitol Building housed both the legislative branch and the judicial branch of government. The executive branch was exiled away from the Capitol Building, to be housed in an executive mansion (not a palace, as possibly some of the more royalist elements in the society preferred to think of it).

This opens up two paradoxical areas in American culture involving technology and tradition. Americans generally love technology. Each generation has embraced the latest and greatest whether it is in hardware or software. The receding generations tend to tolerate change, even if they cannot embrace it for one reason or another. Even the Constitution was designed with change in mind, with the possibility for amendments. The industrial revolution leadership was shared by a few countries but America quickly became its leader. Even the architecture of the new nation took advantage of the latest technologies of buildings—the Capitol Dome has a steel frame while St. Peter's Basilica in Rome, for example, does not.

However, it can be argued that technology is transformative and therefore is clearly part of the concept of revolution. It creates it and prospers by it. It would not take a cultural guru to understand the impact of social networking around the world today or in our nation on governmental homeostasis. Once again, here is where revolution plays a major part in the American people's relationship to their government and to the symbolic representations of government—the public buildings that house those institutions. America was born of revolution. It is in the collective DNA of her citizens. Aggrandizement of the state, through its buildings and architecture, is as culturally, as it is politically, out of touch with the people. America threw away the monarchy and replaced it with an elected government. There is no monarchical tradition or taste-making that motivates the collective public to indulge in beautification of the state as a responsibility of the monarch's "people."

Yet we still want to find a way to create appropriate settings and environments that physically facilitate and even enhance the ability of government to deliver the ideals and precepts of a democratic society, as well as contribute to some form of order, structure, and civility. As technology moves forward all this may once again be revolutionized away by emerging technology as backdrops and settings become virtual and located somewhere in cyberspace. Sir Winston Churchill perhaps articulated the relationship between buildings and people in the most appropriate way: "We shape our buildings and afterwards, our buildings shape us" (Hansard 1943). Of course his perception was pre-information age; however, it still holds remarkably true. Even the design of healthcare facilities, schools, and research and technology centers are designed with the view that the built environment can either enhance or detract from the important activities contained within. Should not the designers of government buildings be similarly challenged?

Now for the paradox. John F. Kennedy, who was arguably one of the most culturally sophisticated presidents in U.S. history, stated the following: "I look forward to an America which will not be afraid of grace and beauty" (1963). This quote is on the west wall of the Kennedy Center for the Performing Arts in Washington, D.C. What did Kennedy mean? He could have said more simply "I love culture and you should too." However, he too recognized our cultural incongruity that embraces technology as revolutionary, and therefore accepted, but design, architecture, and the arts as somehow elitist or even possibly monarchial.

It was during the Kennedy administration that Daniel Patrick Moynihan penned "The Guiding Principles of Federal Architecture," which stated that the U.S. government should "provide requisite facilities in an architectural style and form which is distinguished and which will reflect the dignity, enterprise, vigor, and stability of the American National Government" (1962). This document was written as America was about to rebuild its collective "Main Street," Pennsylvania Avenue, and embark on Kennedy's New Frontier and Lyndon Johnson's Great Society. Unfortunately, Moynihan's writing was much more eloquent and elegant than the 30 years of federal public architecture that ensued. During the Nixon administration, most public architecture became more about expediency and the provision of space for the vastly expanding federal government rather than about vision, purpose, and enablement. However, you had to believe in the positive value of government and its programs to even entertain the notion that you would want to enhance the performance of these institutions or engage the American people in a positive way to appreciate and support them. The headquarters for the Environmental Protection Agency was placed in a leaking, dank, physically unpleasant, leased building, away from the critical mass center of the capital city. Was this the best way to symbolize its permanence, respectability, and importance to the American people?

In 1994 the General Services Administration initiated what became known eventually as the Design Excellence Program. Envisioned at another time of great turmoil in American politics, the goal of the program was to develop an architecture for public buildings that reflected the creativity, inventiveness, strength, and diversity of the American people and that encouraged positive dialogue and mutual respect between the people and their government. In turn, it advocated that our public buildings should enhance not only the performance of the functions contained within but establish environments that encourage mutual respect, self esteem, and purpose for those that lead and administer the government of a democracy, as well as for the citizens who continually facilitate its very existence. It is not the purpose of this essay to evaluate the success or lack of success of the program. Over the past 15 years, or so, there have been some positive and not so positive achievements. However, the basic principles stated at the initiation of the program have remained integral to its execution. Only time will tell whether the buildings did their job and in fact helped move the American experiment in democratic government forward. We judge the value of historic properties in the United States greatly on the age of the building. At 50 years, we consider a building to be eligible for listing on the National Register of Historic Properties, which for a nation that is only slightly more than 200 years old may be considered a long time.

So what will be our legacy to help mark our place in time and in civilization? Buildings and architecture have always contributed greatly to the dialogue between the governors and the governed and between the establishment and the general population. Architecture is a chronicle of the past, the present, and can be projected, by its good or bad influence, on the future. Through all the contradictions and turmoil of the contemporary American experience, what we must leave behind is our commitment to the future of change and to our democracy. Our future in America is predicated on continuing change, born out of revolution but evolving as we move forward. However, this should be based on mutual respect for the people who articulate opinions and ideas that we may not all agree on, but have the right to be heard. In terms of public buildings and architecture, this important work should be accomplished in buildings that enhance and encourage the ongoing development of our collective values, basic ideals, and principles. This is about civility that transcends time and place. It is civility translated into bricks and mortar.

References

Feiner, Edward A., and Marilyn Farley. 2008. "Design Excellence: Building a Public Legacy." In *Architecture: Celebrating the Past, Designing the Future*, edited by Nancy B. Solomon, 240-252. New York: Visual Reference Publications.
Hansard HC Deb 28 October 1943 vol 393 cc403-73.
Kennedy, John F. 1963. *Remarks at Amherst College*, October 26. arts.gov/about/Kennedy.html.
Moynihan, Daniel Patrick. 1962. *Guiding Principles*. Report to the President by the Ad Hoc Committee on Federal Office Space, June 1. moynihansymposium.us/guiding-principles.

IV
Philosophy
and
Ethics

Philosophy and Ethics Themes

Ann Levey, University of Calgary

‖‖‖

For philosophers, what ties together the ideas of civility and democracy is the concept of respect. Each of the three philosophers writing in this volume identifies civility with a kind of respect for others. Joshua Cohen argues that civility is a political virtue that has to do with how we are to argue with each other about political questions. Respect for others in the political arena requires that we listen to others and that we appeal only to the kinds of reasons that can be endorsed by the people with whom we are arguing. Thomas Christiano argues that civility requires that we listen to others and that we respond to them with argument, rather than with heckling or abuse. Like Cohen, he treats civility as primarily a political virtue. Brian Leiter takes civility to be an epistemic virtue. Respecting others, by doing things like listening to them and not abusing or insulting them, promotes knowledge and understanding.

To see why the notion of respect connects civility to democracy it will help to think about what makes democracy a valuable system of government. Philosophers have argued both for and against democracy. Plato thought that democracy was a worse form of government than monarchy or oligarchy because he thought that the average citizen lacked the expertise to make good decisions. For Plato, then, democracy is an epistemically flawed system; it is less likely to produce good decisions about governance than other forms of government because ordinary citizens typically do not know enough to make good decisions. Even if Plato were right about the epistemic point, democracy might have other virtues that make it a desirable form of government. Some people agree with Plato about the epistemic point but think that democracy has virtues other than making better informed decisions.

Many contemporary philosophers endorse democracy because it connects closely to an ideal of equality. Democracy is valuable because it treats people as having an equal say in the rules that govern us. Democracy on this view is a kind of self-government. However, democracy is only a kind of self-government when it involves genuine participation that requires people to listen to each other, respect others' points of view, and be prepared to change their minds in response to the arguments of others. In short, genuine participation requires civility. Christiano's paper emphasizes this connection between democracy and civility. The ideal of democracy requires treating each other as worth listening to in political debate—that is, it requires the virtue of civility.

A very influential understanding of the connection between democracy and civility comes from the work of John Rawls (1993). In Rawls' view, moral equality requires that we not coerce people on the basis of reasons that they could not themselves accept. The idea is that if we use coercion against people for reasons that they could not accept (even if they were reasonable and well-informed) then we treat our own ends and values as more important than theirs. For Rawls, the duty of civility requires more of us than solely that we listen to and try to understand the people with whom we engage in political discourse, at least about fundamental political issues. The Rawlsian duty requires as well that we do not employ as premises in argument reasons that others could not endorse based on the values they hold. Cohen's paper connects civility and democracy through this Rawlsian account of the demands of treating people as moral equals.

A dominant strand in philosophical thinking about democracy, then, focuses on the egalitarian nature of democracy. One might accept this view and agree with Plato that democracy is not a good epistemic method. Cohen, for instance, draws attention to the fact that the Rawlsian duty of civility might require you to sacrifice justice or truth by being willing to compromise with people you think are wrong.

Other philosophers disagree with Plato's epistemic point as well. John Stuart Mill (1862), writing in the nineteenth century, argued that democracy promotes epistemic ends. He disagreed with Plato that democracy is rule by ignorance. Mill argued that the free exchange of ideas is the best method for arriving at the truth because when ideas are debated we can learn from our mistakes and, through this process, false ideas will tend to be replaced with true ideas (Mill 1869). Democracy is a better form of government, Mill thinks, because it requires that one listen to the views of a great number of people, not just the views of a few rulers. Mill's understanding of the epistemic value of democracy helps to show how Brian Leiter's epistemic understanding of civility relates to democracy. According to Leiter's account of civility, democracy will only have the epistemic beneficial effects that Mill supposes if discourse is civil. If discourse is not civil—if the parties don't listen to one another, if they heckle or abuse each other—Mill's conditions for epistemic progress won't be met. Epistemic progress requires that we genuinely listen to others and that we try to engage with their point of view, at least provided they are genuinely engaging with us.

Once we see how the value of democracy relates to civility we see that whether civility is good depends on the circumstances. Where the circumstances of democracy prevail, civility is important for achieving the good of democracy—both the good of moral equality and the good of truth. Both Leiter's and Christiano's papers draw attention to the good of incivility in certain contexts. When one is not otherwise able to be heard, when others are not being honest, sometimes incivility will be necessary to avoid further evils. This in turn raises the question of whether we now live in the circumstances of democracy in which civility is a virtue.

References

Rawls, John. 1993. *Political Liberalism*. New York: Columbia University Press. See especially Lecture VI.

Mill, John Stuart. 1862. *Considerations on Representative Government*. New York: Harper and Brothers. See especially Chapter III.

Mill, John Stuart. 1869. *On Liberty*. London: Longman, Roberts, and Green. See especially Chapter II.

What Is Civility and How Does It Relate to Core Democratic Values?

Thomas Christiano, University of Arizona

||||||||||||||||||||||||||||||||||||||||||||||||||||||||||||||||||||||||||||||||||||||||||||||||||||||||||||||||||||||||||||||||||||||||||||||

C ivility has taken on great importance in contemporary political discussions. Many people think of civility as a very basic norm, the violation of which is responsible for the difficult political impasse we experience today in contemporary politics. We are encouraged to be civil and to avoid incivility. And we are encouraged to think that this will transform the political environment we are in. I am not so sure that incivility is a major factor in explaining our contemporary political predicament. I am not convinced that lack of civility by itself is responsible for the difficult political situation we are in. My inclination is to attribute these difficulties to the rather strong polarization of political opinion and the segregation of persons of different opinions into different political communities. With this segregation comes sloppy ways of thinking about persons in other political groupings and a willingness to engage in rather poor methods of belief formation about other people and their beliefs. I am not saying that incivility is not bad; rather I want to say that it is not the root cause of our present difficulties, as many people seem to think it is.

The Standard Case of Civility

I do not want to give a general definition of "civility" but I will try to focus on a paradigm case of incivility in politics. My aim is to try to understand the idea of civility when it is used in the context of contemporary politics and when it is thought of as a kind of political virtue. I want my elucidation of this common concept to get at some of the key concerns I think are at issue when people are concerned with civility in contemporary politics. I will also propose an account of why civility is a value in a democratic society, which explains why people are upset by the apparent decline in civility.

The central idea of civility is the idea of a negative virtue and an ethical norm (as opposed to a norm applying to institutions or simply to external behavior), consisting of the avoidance of incivility. So I will focus, in what follows, primarily on incivility. Most people are really concerned with the avoidance of incivility when they advocate for greater civility. They may in addition be advocating for positive measures to counteract incivility or even remedies for incivility but the focus is really on incivility.

I will argue that incivility in politics is: (1) inappropriate disruptive interference with someone else's communicative activity; (2) always problematic in some respect; and (3) not always wrong, all things considered. Furthermore I will argue that (4) incivility often has some inherently normative conditions attached to it so it is often (not always) a contestable notion (that is, people may disagree about whether the concept has been properly applied); (5) it is highly contextually determined; and (6) that the value of civility is rooted in the democratic ideal of mutual respect. Perhaps the simplest expression of the view I defend is that incivility is problematic because it amounts to failing to treat one's fellow citizens as equal members of our shared democratic polity by disrupting their ability to communicate their views to the rest of society.

Negative Virtue

Civility is primarily a negative virtue in contemporary discussions. The central concern is with avoiding incivility. Incivility occurs when one person insults, vilifies, heckles, refuses to listen to (in appropriate settings), knowingly interrupts, threatens harm to, treats offensively, or patronizes another person in some context in which this is inappropriate. To treat another civilly is to avoid these forms of action.

The virtue of civility connects action and attitude. John Stuart Mill's idea is that one ought not infer "vices [want of candor, or malignity, bigotry, or intolerance of feeling] from the side which a person takes, though it be the contrary side of the question to our own" (Mill [1859] 1947, 54). More generally, the virtue of civility implies that one avoids making reckless negative inferences about other people's candor. To be uncivil is to act in the above ways toward other persons on the basis of reckless reasoning about those others and their ideas. This is the most general way of characterizing incivility. Now let us consider some details.

General Characterization of the Paradigm Case of Incivility in Politics

A standard case of incivility in politics is a kind of inappropriate disruptive interference with another person's ability to communicate and be taken seriously. Uncivil behavior can interfere physically with a person's ability to speak or with an audience's ability to hear. The intentional interruptions, heckling, shouting, and threatening behavior are designed simply to stop the other from talking or from being heard. Alternatively, uncivil behavior can interfere with the person's receiving a fair hearing by undermining the credibility of the speaker. Insults, vilification, and mockery under certain circumstances (and when particularly intense) are ways of undermining the speaker by causing he or she to not be taken seriously by the audience. To the extent that it does this, incivility seems to cut against the democratic ideal of giving each person a fair hearing in the process of political discussion.

Normative Conditions

Attributions of incivility are often contestable because an assertion that someone has acted uncivilly usually involves some statement that the person has violated a norm of reasoning or fair dealing. For example, in some contexts, saying that someone has acted stupidly when the description is unquestionably justified does not seem to be a case of incivility. It is only a case of incivility when there is some reasonable disagreement among participants about the characterization. In some contexts, vilifying a person need not be uncivil if the person is genuinely a villain in the sense in which the person who is making the attribution means it. Calling a person corrupt or a liar is not a case of incivility in some contexts in which the person genuinely, reasonably, and uncontroversially merits the description. But calling a person a liar where the evidence is unclear or controversial seems to be a case of incivility. Of course, racist, sexist, and ethnic slurs are always uncivil when they are adopted for the purpose of disruption because they are always unjust and indefensible.

In some cases, attributions of incivility are contestable. For example, someone can think that they are not acting uncivilly because they think they have good reason to vilify another person. Sometimes, such an action can still be uncivil if it betrays a reckless unconcern for the evidence. For example, someone who calls another a liar simply because they disagree with the person and because they make some vague association of the person's ideas with lying is being uncivil even if they do sincerely think the other is lying and think they have evidence for it. If the evidence is inadequate or is recklessly used as a basis of inference, then the action is uncivil. Or someone who employs highly questionable inferences to connect the appearance of the speaker or his or her views to a judgment about the speaker's corruption is being uncivil even if they would not accept the characterization because they think they speak the truth. Again, contrast this case of inadequately based attributions of corruption with attributions of corruption that have been held up by reasonably unbiased courts of law. The latter are not necessarily uncivil, the former nearly always are.

These cases of incivility include both mental conditions and action. The mental condition involves the aim of disruption or at least the unconcern with disruption and the recklessness of the charges. The actions are insults, heckling, and ignoring another. Unlike defamation, truth is not always a defense. This is because incivility is essentially an ethical condition and concerns ethical norms. It is not merely a matter of external action.

Obviously there will be some disagreement about when the evidence is adequate to support such a charge or when someone has been negligent. And differing assessments of these can lead to charges and countercharges of incivility.

There are some other normative conditions that hold for civility. Even if one is justified in asserting a person is a liar, one may still have to wait one's turn to say it and one may still be obligated to refrain from interrupting the person. If one has a fair turn at expressing one's views, it is problematic to interrupt another, even if one's charges are well grounded. There is also some kind of norm that the information is transmitted in a way that allows reasoned assessment. Screaming one's views or articulating them in a way that is intentionally provocative or manipulative may also constitute uncivil activity to the extent that one is undermining the other person's ability to think clearly about what is being said.

This assumes, of course, that one has an adequate opportunity to make the charge that in some way equals the importance of it. And it also assumes that reasoned assessment is not precluded by the circumstances. We need to ask whether a highly disruptive activity of heckling or insults is a case of incivility if the insults are justified and if one is somehow unfairly excluded from the ordinary processes of discussion. My inclination is to think that at least some actions that would normally be deemed uncivil are not in fact uncivil if the supposedly uncivil action is the only way a person or group can express itself due to the fact that they are unfairly excluded from the public forum. I will discuss these conditions a bit later. But here again, as one can see readily, there will be significant disagreements about whether the normative conditions of proper reasoning and fair access are met.

Some Kind of *Pro Tanto* Reason against Incivility

There is always something amiss when one person treats another uncivilly, though incivility need not be the wrong thing to do, all things considered in all circumstances. This is similar to a kind of presumption against breaking a promise or damaging someone's property. These are generally morally problematic but they can sometimes be justified. If I have promised someone that I would meet them for lunch, but on the way to my appointment I find a person who is in desperate need and who only I can help, I will be justified in missing my lunch appointment.

Not Always the Wrong Thing to Do, All Things Considered

Even when incivility is problematic, it may be right to act uncivilly if the speech of the interfered-with person is sufficiently oppressive or stupid or malignant. It may also be the right thing to do if the person's speech will lead to very bad or unjust results that cannot be or are very unlikely to be avoided after the speech. Here the evident bad of incivility is outweighed by the great weight of the moral good pursued.

This possible justification of incivility may lead to serious problems in a highly polarized society in which each group sees the actions of the other group as highly destructive. People may come to think that treating others uncivilly is justified in order to avoid disaster.

Heavily Contextually Determined

Knowingly interrupting a person is normally uncivil but it need not be in some cases. For example, where the interrupter has authority to do it, it is not uncivil for the authority to interrupt. Or in a highly cooperative intellectual enterprise where people are trying to get the right answer and they are brainstorming, they may interrupt each other quite a bit without being uncivil. Yet, here too if someone does it too much it is uncivil.

Even the association between heckling and incivility is sometimes contextually determined. Booing in the House of Commons is not considered uncivil; it is normal. On the other hand, the screaming and abusive language of Nazi judges in courts in which anti-Nazi dissidents were tried seems clearly to be a case of institutionalized or normalized incivility. So the mere fact that some kind of behavior is in accordance with widely accepted norms does not entail that it is not uncivil.

Civility and the Democratic Idea of Mutual Respect

We can put the above theses together now and try to explain them by reference to a deeper idea. I think the key value that is usually at stake in discussions of civility in politics is the democratic value of mutual respect. When norms of civility in democratic politics are violated, it is usually because the actions at issue seem to betray some failure of respect on the part of some citizens for fellow citizens, which respect they are duty bound to have and express. Interestingly, it is often the case that the people who seem to fail in this way do not think they have violated any duty of respect for fellow citizens.

It is difficult to give a clear characterization of what this mutual respect consists of. But perhaps the best way to characterize the worry about incivility is by reference to an ideal of democratic discussion and deliberation. The ideal is one in which each person listens to the proposals and arguments of others and considers them on the merits and then responds with agreement or with counterarguments and counterproposals with arguments to defend them. When disagreement becomes intractable and decisions must be made, different persons propose compromises and arguments for them. There are negotiations and further proposed compromises and arguments. At some point, enough people accept some particular compromise and decide accordingly.

In this process each person listens carefully to all comers and evaluates the arguments and proposals according to the merits of the proposals. This is a circumstance in which there is no incivility. Each person respects every other person. Each person listens and considers. And each person is treated as having a point of view worth listening to. The respect has to be mutual, so when a person has finished his or her arguments and everyone has heard them, he or she steps away and lets others give their arguments. Unnecessary repetition is avoided and everyone has a chance to have a say. This is an ideal of mutual and equal respect.

Each person accords the other the benefit of the doubt that they are conscientious participants and not motivated by gain or foolishness. This is what John Rawls calls the implications of the burdens of judgment (Rawls 1993). We recognize that disagreement can arise from the conscientious efforts of all parties. Only strong evidence can overcome this benefit of the doubt in public.

This picture of ideal democratic deliberation and the mutual respect that it manifests gives us a way of explaining the different components of civility that I have given above. It explains what civility has to do with the protection of reasoned communication between persons. It explains also why civility has to include action as well as attitude and reasoning, because action can express a lack of respect when it is connected with attitudes and reasoning in a certain way. It also explains the normative conditions on civility, since if one does not have fair access to public discussion it is hard to see how one is violating democratic norms by interrupting. It explains why civility is a value since it is connected to a central democratic value. It also explains why the value of civility can be overridden since democracy and the mutual respect among persons are not the only values at stake in a discussion. The connection of civility to mutual respect in a democracy also explains why some charges of villainy, deception, corruption, etc. are not uncivil, as long as they are delivered in the right way. When the charge is well grounded, the targeted person has already violated the norm of mutual respect. They have forfeited the usual benefit of the doubt that we normally have reason to accord to each participant. Trying to barge into a discussion (by means of interruption) from which one is improperly excluded may not be uncivil. But heckling is always uncivil (though it may not always be wrong). Of course one may interrupt a person simply to stop them from saying the same thing for the thousandth time. This needn't be uncivil; it need not imply that the person's point of view is of no account.

Incivility

Now let us step away from this ideal little by little. First, even in a circumstance in which every proposer and arguer deserves a full hearing, in the societies we know, even the most engaged people cannot absorb all of the arguments from every point of view. Second, most people in the world we live in cannot afford the time or the energy to listen to all these meritorious ideas. People have limited cognitive space to listen and comprehend alternative ideas. At some point, most people turn away from what others have to say. They pay no attention. They cannot be blamed for this because they have day jobs, families, lives, etc. to attend to. People stop listening, but they show no lack of respect or incivility. They simply have to move on to other things.

Incivility short-circuits the process of discussion described above, not because one has no more time but because one sees the other as not worth listening to. In the idealized process everyone patiently listens to everyone else and waits his or her turn to speak; it is assumed that their turn will come about and that everyone else will listen then. There are various ways in which this can be undermined. One person may talk so long that others do not get their chance. One person may try to interfere with the speech of another by heckling, talking over them, or interrupting them. One person may interfere with another by trying without adequate evidence to undercut the person's credibility with others.

Incivility seems to display a lack of respect toward a fellow citizen. It says that the person has nothing of worth to say either because they are liars, idiots, corrupt, childish, or foolish. But normally incivility does not attempt merely to stop the person from repetition. Usually it attempts to silence the person altogether or make sure that no one takes them seriously. It suggests that the point of view is of no account or ought to be suppressed. It undermines that person's ability to address the community by making communication very difficult or by undermining the respect necessary to take what that person says seriously.

Enclaves and the Climate of Incivility

Not all use of abusive language or vilification is uncivil. If it is carried out in enclaves where opinions are formed and dissident ideas are allowed to flourish, this need not be uncivil. Incivility, I think, has primarily to do with disruption of another's speech or communication.

To be sure, vilification, abuse, and other such things can contribute to a climate of incivility: a climate in which charges of this sort are too easily bandied about or in which people think it is appropriate to shout other people down. Incivility is often the result of polarization of groups in which people within a group develop very strong beliefs about those in the other group. They do not feel constrained by the duty that one not interpret disagreement with others as a consequence of the immorality, stupidity, or mendacity of the other.

This suggests one of the dilemmas of the use of vilification and abuse in politics. Sometimes in enclaves, reckless and abusive characterizations of others can be useful and even defensible behaviors as long as the members of the group do not take the abuse too seriously or so seriously that they then feel justified in publicly broadcasting the abuse. Hyperbole, excess, and other such things are often necessary in politics to build solidarity and give a sense of courage and mission. I think this kind of thing is particularly defensible with oppressed people. The problem arises when people take this too seriously and begin to believe these things literally and then begin to act on them. This produces reckless belief formation and a sense of alienation from others.

Non-Ideal Circumstances

Obviously we don't live in the ideal democratic circumstances I described above. Even so, many of the norms of civility apply in non-ideal circumstances as long as they are not too remote from the ideal. But they don't always win out. We live under circumstances in which many persons are treated very badly and in which persons are not accorded respect and are marginalized and hated. Or some people are not treated with the respect they deserve as in the case of a society still pervaded with racism and sexism and various kinds of ethnic hatred. We live in circumstances in which some unpopular opinions are the objects of invective and are marginalized and vilified (antiwar protests often have this character). Sometimes institutions marginalize and sometimes it is just the climate of opinion and feeling in a society. These may not result in uncivil behavior. They may be sufficiently widespread opinions or pervasive institutions that no one needs to act uncivilly. Those who are closed out in these circumstances, who do not have institutional power and who do not have the general climate of opinion behind them, can only be heard by barging in and being disruptive.

This is a cruel irony of the norm of civility. The deeply oppressive groups and activities in the society appear not to be uncivil while those who rightly protest against them seem to be or are violating the norms of civility. The background institutions are deeply unjust but their injustice is in the background for most people. They only notice the apparent or actual incivility of the people who are in fact oppressed and whose only recourse is disruptive behavior.

In some of these cases, there is no incivility because the purportedly uncivil persons are not being accorded sufficient space in the public sphere and their interventions are merely taking space they are owed. My guess is that many in the southern United States perceived the civil rights movement as being uncivil because the activities of marching and chanting were not the normal avenues for political expression, especially not for African Americans. They were seen as disruptive activities designed to provoke angry responses. These are contextual norms for the political environment. We do not see the civil rights movement in that way partly because we do not share the same norms. Protests and demonstrations in public spaces are accepted forms of politics in the modern world, partly due to the influence of the civil rights movement and its success in achieving significant social change without violence. But, most important, we can see that the activities of marching and chanting in public places were the only avenue of expression for people who were excluded from the public sphere in many different ways. African Americans did not have access to the political sphere and so violation of norms in this context was justified and not uncivil.

In other cases there may be incivility but it is nevertheless justified by the weight of the concerns that the uncivil behavior is meant to promote. In these cases, incivility can be somewhat like civil disobedience. It would still be better if the oppression could be responded to in a respectful and democratic manner, so there is something lost. But it is, all things considered, defensible behavior.

The Problem of Incivility

From a political standpoint, these justifications can pose difficulties because of their highly contestable character. Many groups in contemporary society cultivate strong senses of grievance and injustice. To the extent that this occurs in a highly polarized society it is a basis for serious conflict. When opposing groups nurse this sense of grievance or injustice, each often thinks that the other group is acting without justification. So the norms that justify incivility or that annul the charge of incivility are ones that can be invoked by many groups, and many other groups will see them as unjustified in their incivility. For example, some elements of the pro-life movement in the United States often describe abortion as morally similar to the Holocaust or to slavery in the antebellum South. The comparison, if correct, would certainly justify heckling or vilifying pro-choice activists, abortion providers, and women who have had abortions. Presumably this would be on par with the justification of heckling Nazis or slaveholders. It may be uncivil but it might be justified overall because of the weight of the evil that is opposed.

Furthermore, the more society is polarized around different views and segregated into groups that have these very different views, the greater is the ability of people to think of persons of other persuasions as traitors, liars, murderers, and generally corrupt defenders of the indefensible. Under these circumstances, the justification of incivility or the sense that one is not acting uncivilly, even while shouting down one's fellow citizens or vilifying them, can become quite widespread. To the charge that one is failing to treat one's fellow citizens with equal respect, the response might be, "So what?" or "They deserve it!" or "Just look at what *they* are doing!"

Without the extremist views and without the sloppy and emotionally charged reasoning about others that goes into much of contemporary politics, it is hard to see how there would be much incivility. It is these phenomena that tempt people into thinking that their fellow citizens do not deserve equal respect and to act accordingly.

So it seems to me that it is not incivility that is the root problem; it is a mere symptom of another deeper set of problems that explain the polarization of our society and the willingness of citizens to look at each other as criminals. It is these phenomena that need to be attacked. To see this, notice that we are not likely to get people to change their behaviors by pointing to the norm of civility, because they often already think they are acting civilly or are justifiably overriding the norm of civility. And given the contestable nature of charges of incivility, this response may make sense. They simply think that the opposing group is oppressing them and that they are therefore justified in disrupting the activities of the opposing group. What we need most urgently to do is get people to see each other as equal citizens who are conscientiously disagreeing on difficult issues.

To be sure, there may be circumstances where we bring someone who holds extremist views, which commit them to not treating their fellow citizens as equal members of the polity, to see what they are doing. And this might lead them in some cases to moderate their positions. It may also be the case that sometimes rather moderate disagreement can become the fuel for deeply uncivil behavior. In these kinds of cases, a reminder to each of the parties that their opposites are equal citizens deserving of respect may be what is needed. But I am not convinced that this is what is fueling much of the current climate of incivility.

Conclusion

I have defended a conception of a standard case of civility and I have argued that the value of political civility is grounded in the democratic ideal of equal respect among fellow citizens. I conclude that incivility is not a root cause of the problems we are currently experiencing. Though civility is grounded in a fundamental democratic value, the absence of civility in contemporary politics is more a symptom of other problems such as polarization, extremism, and enclave group thinking than a genuine cause of the current difficulties.

References

Mill, John Stuart. (1859) 1947. *On Liberty.* Northbrook, IL: AHM Publishing Corporation.
Rawls, John. 1993. *Political Liberalism.* New York: Columbia University Press.

Reflections on Civility

Joshua Cohen, Stanford University

I am going to offer some reflections on civility and on the place of civility in a democracy. My reflections are organized around three questions:
1. What is civility?
2. What are some of civility's benefits?
3. What are some of civility's costs?

There is of course a fourth question: do the benefits of civility outweigh the costs? The answer depends on context, and I will leave the exploration of the precise nature of that contextual dependence for another occasion.

1. What is civility?

That is a large question and the answer is much contested. So we need some focus. I will provide focus by drawing on some ideas from John Rawls—in particular from Rawls's *Political Liberalism* (1996). That book addresses a very large issue: how can we live together in a reasonably just, democratic society, given our profound disagreements—disagreements of interest, disagreements in ideas about justice, and disagreements in our philosophical, moral, and religious convictions?

As one part of a much more complicated answer, Rawls argues that we need to respect a "duty of civility" (217, 236). The duty of civility, he says, is not a legal duty; you don't get punished for violating it. Moreover, it is not a duty in our personal lives, nor a duty throughout our social lives. It is not about how we talk to our friends or students or members of our neighborhood or church or union or company. It is not about politeness and etiquette.

To appreciate the point, consider the "Rules of Civility and Decent Behavior," copied by George Washington when he was 16 years old. As it turns out, George Washington was the Miss Manners of the late 18th century. Here are some of his rules of civility:

> Lift not one eyebrow higher than another, wry not the mouth, and bedew no man's face with your spittle, by approaching too near him when you speak.

> Be not tedious in discourse, make not many digressions, nor repeat often the same manner of discourse. (2008)

Unlike Washington's duty of civility, Rawls's is about politics. It is, in particular, about how we ought to argue with others on basic political and constitutional questions. In particular, the duty of civility requires two things of us.

First, that we be prepared to explain to others why the laws that we support can be supported by values and principles that those other people can endorse: by public values and principles that lie on common ground—say, values of liberty, equality, and the general welfare.

Second, that we listen to others and be open to accommodating their views.

To explain the idea, consider some examples of cases in which one violates the duty of civility. It is a violation of the duty of civility when you defend a law or policy and all you can say in support of the law or policy is:

There should be Sunday closing laws because that is when God fixed the Sabbath.

There should be no abortion after 18 weeks because God ensouls the fetus at quickening.

There should be no gay marriage because "in the Creator's plan, sexual complementarity and fruitfulness belong to the very nature of marriage" (Ratzinger 2003).

There should be no legal enforcement of morality because the basis of right and wrong is the autonomy of personal judgment.

There should be equal political rights because the life of political activity is the best human life.

Civil disobedience is permissible because unjust "laws" violate God's law and thus are not really laws at all, and impose no obligation of compliance.

If you accept the duty of civility, you do not rest the case for your political conclusions on these arguments, even if you think the arguments are perfectly sound and valid. The problem is that the arguments appeal to contentious comprehensive religious and moral doctrines, not simply to political ideas that might provide common ground. The duty of civility, as I am describing it, imposes demands of self-restraint that such appeals violate.

Let us pause for a moment to consider an objection. You might object that this conception of the duty of civility is misguided because it implies that Martin Luther King Jr. violated the duty of civility when he wrote the following words in his letter from the Birmingham jail:

A just law is a man-made code that squares with moral law or the law of God. An unjust law is a code that is out of harmony with the moral law. To put it in the terms of St. Thomas Aquinas: An unjust law is a human law that is not rooted in eternal law and natural law. (1963)

This objection is misguided. King did not violate the duty of civility when he wrote those words, because he had a few other things to say as well—other things that invoke public values and principles. In particular, he also said:

> One day the South will know that when these disinherited children of God sat down at lunch counters, they were in reality standing up for what is best in the American dream and for the most sacred values in our Judaeo-Christian heritage, thereby bringing our nation back to those great wells of democracy which were dug deep by the founding fathers in their formulation of the Constitution and the Declaration of Independence. (1963)

Here, like Frederick Douglas and Abraham Lincoln, King is reading the Constitution through the Declaration of Independence, with its conception of human beings as created equal. And in his letter, King also said:

> An unjust law is a code that a numerical or power majority group compels a minority group to obey but does not make binding on itself. This is difference made legal… A law is unjust if it is inflicted on a minority that, as a result of being denied the right to vote, had no part in enacting or devising the law. (1963)

King did not violate the duty of civility, as I described it, by making a Thomistic statement about unjust laws being no laws at all, thus imposing no obligations, because he had these other things to say as well.

2. What are the benefits of civility?

I come now to the second question. Three considerations speak in favor of the duty of civility. I will call them, respectively, reasons of equality, humility, and political inclusion.

One reason for endorsing and acting on the duty of civility is that by doing so you treat other citizens as equals. You reject the idea that politics is a kind of private property, owned by you and the people you agree with. You treat others as equal members of "We, The People" by constructing political justifications that respect the duty of civility by operating on common ground.

You also show a kind of humility. When you respect the duty of civility, you still think that your basic principles are right, but you also acknowledge that you might be wrong. You acknowledge that reasonable people might disagree with you, and you look to work on common ground that reasonable people can all accept.

And third, arguing on common ground is inclusive. Think of movements against slavery, for religious toleration, for extending suffrage, against racial apartheid, against subordination of women, against class domination, and for universal human rights. All these of movements have been animated by an ideal of inclusion: all reject the idea that some people count for nothing. By looking for common ground, you are being inclusive in the democratic community by offering reasons that are not so plainly sectarian, that others have reason to endorse.

3. What are some costs of civility?

This brings me to the third question. You might say, "Costs? Isn't civility all nice and warm and cozy?" No, it is not. The duty of civility requires a kind of self-restraint, which is, to all appearances, not easy. What, more particularly, are some of the costs of the self-restraint imposed by the duty of civility?

First, you may end up sacrificing justice because part of the duty of civility is a willingness to accommodate. And after all, when you accommodate, you are accommodating people who you think are wrong, who hold views that you think are wrong. So that is one potential cost.

A second cost is that you may sacrifice truth by being willing to accommodate, which is not to suggest that you will say something that you think is false, but that you will, as part of the self-restraint demanded by the duty of civility, not present everything that you think is true. Not because you think it is not really true: you think it is true, but you think it is inappropriate in a political community of equals to offer that particular justification for law and policy that is intended to command the respect of all.

So you might sacrifice justice, you might sacrifice some truth, and, third, you may be played for a sucker. You might be played for a sucker by being civil to others who are not being civil, even though they may be pretending to be civil—played for a sucker for being civil to others (thus being self-restrained) who are not being civil in return.

Here is an expression of this concern, which comes from Don Feder, writing in *Front Page*. He says:

> The left has perfected the gentle art of character assassination, while complaining about the politics of personal destruction. Their idea of a civilized dialogue is calling us really-mean Nazis, while our mouths are taped shut. (2006)

I am neither endorsing nor criticizing this point; just offering it as an example of the worry about being taken for a sucker.

There may, then, be costs to civility—to respecting the duty of civility. And that brings me to question four: do the benefits outweigh the costs? And, if so, when, under what circumstances? What is the right balance? That, as I said, depends on context; I will leave the nature of the contextual dependence for another occasion.

References

Feder, Don, 2006. "A Taste of Left-Wing 'Civility.'" *FrontPage Magazine*, June 23. archive. frontpagemag.com/readArticle.aspx?ARTID=3853.

King, Martin Luther, Jr. 1963. "Letter from Birmingham Jail." April 16. mlk-kpp01.stanford. edu/index.php/encyclopedia/documentsentry/annotated_letter_from_birmingham.

Ratzinger, Joseph. 2003. "The Vatican on Homosexual Marriage." June 3. www.vatican. va/roman_curia/congregations/cfaith/documents/rc_con_cfaith_doc_20030731_ homosexual-unions_en.html.

Rawls, John, 1996. *Political Liberalism*. New York: Columbia University Press.

Washington, George. 2008. *George Washington's Rules of Civility and Decent Behavior*. Naperville, IL: Sourcebooks.

The Circumstances of Civility

Brian Leiter, University of Chicago

W hat are the circumstances in which civility in discourse is both necessary and obligatory? By "civility in discourse" I mean observing a variety of norms about language, tone, and attitude governing an exchange of words and ideas: for example, showing respect for the other person or persons with whom one is conversing; avoiding insulting, demeaning, or derisive language (or gestures); and genuinely listening to (and trying to make good sense of) what the other person says.[1] I shall assume that, pre-theoretically, everyone can agree that "civility" is paramount for discourse in the classroom setting. Teachers should be civil to students, and students to their teachers. So let us start with that case and examine why civility seems so obviously important in that context.

In the first instance, the teacher has an overriding pedagogical obligation; namely, to help the students understand the material being taught. Understanding is impeded by uncivil language from the teacher toward the student. Insults, disparaging or derisive remarks, or expressions of contempt make their targets defensive, alienated, and angry. It is hard to see how such a response is conducive to learning and understanding. But why should students be civil to the teacher or to their fellow students? I put aside the obviously self-interested reasons for avoiding incivility, such as receiving a lower mark from the teacher. Surely the real reasons for civility of students toward teachers and fellow students derive, again, from the obligations of those who wish to acquire knowledge and understanding. Just as the teacher has an obligation, deriving from pedagogical duty, to insure that the student is, both cognitively and affectively, maximally able to understand and learn, so the students have such obligations to each other and the teacher, for without their commitment to civility, the ends of education will not be realized.

Of course, the pedagogical situation has another important feature—an inequality in knowledge and competence (in the subject matter) between teacher and students. This is why civility toward students is so important, since students recognize the inequality in competence and, at the same time, are almost certain to make mistakes, sometimes serious mistakes, in their comments and questions. Yet such mistakes, and the appreciation of them as mistakes, are often an important part of the reliable acquisition of knowledge and understanding—a point emphasized by many writers in our philosophical tradition, from Socrates to Mill. But only in an educational atmosphere marked by civility will students likely take the risk of making mistakes, and only in such an atmosphere are they likely to be able to learn from the mistakes. If the mistakes, and the inequality in competence that is their source, are an occasion for mockery and demeaning comments, then, again, the pedagogical goals will likely be defeated.

Notice, then, that in the classroom the circumstances of civility include the aim of imparting knowledge and understanding, a recognized inequality of competence between teacher and learner, the need for learners to have the opportunity to make mistakes and learn from those mistakes, and the interest learners have in acquiring knowledge and understanding. The circumstances of civility, in short, involve essentially what I will refer to as epistemic values and motives: knowledge, understanding, learning, and the desire for all of these. (I suspect the recognized inequality in competence is not essential to the circumstances of civility, though it is a feature of the classroom situation.) In circumstances where epistemic values and motives govern, civility is essential and should be considered obligatory.[2]

What then of the realm of politics, our real concern in the context of this conference? Politics, at least in nominally democratic societies, does not have as its primary aim knowledge and understanding. The primary aims of politics are practical—for example, how to govern our collective life and how to allocate the benefits and burdens of communal existence. Knowledge and understanding, however, play an essential instrumental role in the ultimately practical decisions that we must take in politics, and thus much of political discourse in fact concerns what we know and what is true: will, for example, government-run healthcare improve health outcomes for most people or not, will it control medical costs or not, and so on. So in politics, as in the classroom, one of the ends is knowledge and understanding, at least the kind of knowledge and understanding necessary for practical decisions.

But are epistemic values paramount in the political arena, as they are in the classroom? In politics, most obviously, there does not appear to be an acknowledged inequality of competence between teachers and learners in a democratic polity—even though there are clearly inequalities of competence aplenty, though not necessarily between citizens and elected officials. Nor is it clear that there is necessarily an interest in learning from mistakes, or even a shared interest in knowledge and understanding. In the realm of

politics, sometimes the non-epistemic interests affected by a practical decision dominate all the epistemic interests.

Let us describe, then, a political situation in which the circumstances
of civility quite clearly do not pertain. I shall call this political situation
Dystopia. In Dystopia, let us assume that political leaders and citizens do
not speak honestly, do not state their actual reasons or evidence, and are
wholly motivated by non-epistemic considerations, such as personal gain
or gain for their group (however that group is defined). Political leaders
and their followers do not acknowledge mistakes, since that would be a
sign of weakness, and they regularly subordinate epistemic considerations
to non-epistemic ones, believing to be true whatever is most useful to those
non-epistemic interests and smearing or dismissing anyone who brings to
bear actual epistemic values.

Unsurprisingly, in Dystopia those who are not interested in knowledge
and understanding are very concerned with being treated with civility, because
they have noticed that those who are treated with civility have moral and
epistemic status. This is an important point about civility: we only treat
civilly those who have some reasonable claim on informing our moral and
epistemic decisions. Those recognized as craven villains, moral miscreants,
or pathological liars have no claim on civil treatment. We would not think
that it is a failing in civility if the conference on civility and democracy, that,
for example, simply ignored the Nazi view that civility is a Jewish device
for controlling the world. Nor would it seem a culpable failing of civility
in Weimar Germany in 1930 for democrats and anti-fascists to vigorously
condemn the Nazis, to shout them down and deride them as vicious bigots
with a monstrous agenda.[3] As the economists like to say, civility is a signaling
device: if you are treated with civility, then you must be a person with status
in the community, such that your input into matters epistemic or practical counts. But in Dystopia, the most strident demands from civility come
from those who have no actual entitlement to moral or epistemic credibility.

It is enough to create a Dystopia that only one significant political party
has the characteristics described above. If all parties to political life are Dystopic in the ways described, then all parties will have a self-interest in civility,
as a cover for their actual objectives. But the hard, and really frightening,
case of Dystopia is one in which some parties to public life genuinely want
to acquire knowledge and understanding in order to make good practical
decisions about communal life, while some other party or parties are fully
Dystopic. We can expect, as noted, that the Dysoptic parties will be interested
in civility, but the real question is whether the other parties have an obligation

to be civil toward them, given that they have so fully subordinated epistemic values and motives to non-epistemic and self-serving ends.

That the conditions of civility do not obtain—as they do not in Dystopia—means there is no obligation of civility, but it does not necessarily mean that we ought to be uncivil. The question, now, reduces to a purely instrumental one. Perhaps, even in Dystopia, civility is a more effective means for exposing the hypocrisy or ulterior agendas of one's political opponents. But that is a complicated question about political psychology and sociology. It might turn out that in Dystopia, the best defense for those concerned with epistemic values—as well as the good and the right—is derisive remarks and insulting polemics. There is precious little empirical evidence, after all, that moral or political attitudes are strongly influenced by dispassionate, discursive reasoning, so it might be that in Dystopia civility is not only not obligatory but not even advisable, given other important moral objectives, such as the discovery of the truth and the promotion of what is just. I cannot hope to settle that question here; I want only to suggest that in Dystopia, there is no obligation of civility and that its desirability depends on an answer to psychological questions about its effects.

One final, and obviously timely, question remains: is the United States today more like Dystopia or more like a society in which the circumstances of civility obtain? One might be forgiven for thinking that it is increasingly like the former rather than the latter. But to settle that question would require an exploration of history and politics that go beyond the purview of this brief philosophical inquiry into the ordinary notion of civility and its circumstances.[4]

Notes

1. There is a technical sense of "civility" that has arisen within the later Rawlsian approach to political philosophy, according to which citizens have a moral duty to only offer reasons in the public sphere that are acceptable to all. (The approach is well-discussed by Joshua Cohen in his contribution to this volume.) This has only a little to do with the ordinary notion of civility, and in any case is predicated on an unrealizable ideal, as the many critics of the later Rawls have noted. So I will ignore that somewhat idiosyncratic sense of "civility" here.

2. Civility plays other roles in our social life unrelated to epistemic values, such as easing the superficial social interactions characteristic of human life. Civility has value in these contexts, to be sure, but I am less sure it should be considered obligatory.

3. Some philosophers with Kantian intuitions think that civility is always a general requirement of respect for persons, an intuition that I do not share, and for which I cannot think of any compelling arguments, and many objectionable counter-examples, like those in the text: treating Nazis in Weimar Germany with civility seems to me a moral failing on the

part of their opponents, not a requirement of respect. Such a demanding conception of civility would also be incompatible with derisive polemics (think H.L. Mencken), which often play an important role in political and social life.

4. My thanks to Martha Nussbaum for feedback on an earlier draft and to my co-panelists at the March 4 conference, Tom Christiano and Joshua Cohen, for the stimulus of their remarks. My thanks, finally, to members of the audience for their useful questions.

V
Communication
and
Media

Introduction:
Media and Civility in Context

Lawrence Pintak, Washington State University

'm standing in the cell where they held me for three months and I can't stop sobbing."

That was gist of a tweet sent by a Cairo blogger. It was March 5, 2011, the day Egyptian activists stormed the capital's State Security building in the ongoing revolution that had toppled Hosni Mubarak. I was sitting in a seminar room 10,000 miles away riveted to my iPad as a rapid-fire series of tweets scrolled out real-time from bloggers, activists, and journalists I had known for years.

Around me, American political activists, policymakers, and academics bemoaned the state of U.S. democracy, while, on my iPad, messages from their Egyptian counterparts described the scenes playing out as they rummaged through long-secret files—including their own—and the pain-filled torture chambers of the dying regime.

The juxtaposition of the National Endowment for the Humanities conference on civility and democracy in the Pacific Northwest and the simultaneous drama taking place in Cairo were both a reminder that incivility is a relative thing and that democracy and freedom are tenuous privileges to be nurtured and protected.

In three decades covering wars, revolutions, coups, and terrorism on four continents, I have witnessed firsthand what happens to human beings when the structures of civility collapse. And as a journalist, I know the power of the media to fan the flames of conflict. Which was why, returning to the United States from the Middle East two years before the conference, I had been stuck by how polarized our society had become, and concerned about the role the media had played in bringing us to that point. The shooting of Representative Gail Gifford not long before the civility and democracy conference was but the latest example of the bitter divisions that have gripped the American body politic.

On one level, American politics have become more democratized than ever before. Talk radio, social media, blogs, and all the rest mean that the "silent majority" is a relic of history. Anyone and everyone can—and, it sometimes seems, does—express their opinions about the issues of the day. That's a wonderful thing. But it also means we no longer have a national narrative or a shared worldview.

Back in the 1970s, Spiro Agnew fulminated against the "nattering nabobs of negativism" among the elite who controlled the media agenda ("Remembering Agnew" 1996). Whether or not Agnew had a point about their politics, he was right that the news agenda was largely written by a handful of influential journalists in New York and Washington, D.C. But that also meant we had a shared view of the world. Each evening, a third of all Americans gathered around their TVs and saw the world according to Uncle Walter—Cronkite, of course—and his counterparts at NBC and ABC. Today, we have a plethora of news sources to choose from: *New York Times* to *Drudge Report*, Fox News to *The Daily Show*, Rush Limbaugh to a blog run by some kid down the street. To put it mildly, not all of them are created equal. Opinion, not objectivity, is the currency of the day. Facts give way to factoids. There are fewer and fewer journalists actually reporting the news and more and more people analyzing, parsing, and spinning the information to fit their own agenda.

As Bill Keller, then editor of the *New York Times*, observed, the web may offer a tsunami of blogs and information aggregators, but "what's absent from this vast array of new media outlets is, first and foremost, the great engine of news gathering—the people who witness events, ferret out information, supply context and information" (Preston 2007).

And, since we're human, many of us just turn to the sources that reinforce our preconceived notions. Shared worldview gives way to twisted silos—and to twisted politics, not just because we don't have the facts to make intelligent decisions. With the birth of 24/7 cable news in 1980, there was much talk of the "CNN effect," the idea that policymakers at the White House and State Department were being forced to react in real-time when crises broke abroad, while they previously had a full news cycle to weigh their options. Instead of spurring premature action, today's "new media effect" has introduced paralysis into the political system. Lawmaking used to be about deal-making and compromise; today, members of Congress live in fear of provoking a backlash from the bloggers—no matter which side of the aisle. Better not to make a decision than to make—what is inevitably perceived by someone as—the wrong one.

At the same time, our new media landscape plays to the extremes. Controversy generates audience, so the most extreme views get the most attention on the web, and quickly morph up through the media ecosphere to cable television and mainstream papers. Just look at the hours of coverage devoted to an obscure fringe preacher from Florida who announced he was going to burn a Qur'an.

The more outrageous the comment or action, the greater chance the quote or image will instantly streak across the Internet and echo from television sets. Ultimate Fighting—for which Fox is paying the league $100 million annually—meets American politics.

"He said, she said" journalism has degenerated into "I said" journalism as so many reporters tell us what we should think instead of letting us decide for ourselves. Television "news" programs have become a showcase for hosts to vent their made-for-TV outrage in response to ever more extreme and bizarre guests. Witness Anderson Cooper's weeklong tirade against some obscure Texas state legislator's unsubstantiated claims that Muslims were having babies in America, taking them home to be trained as *jihadis*, then infiltrating them back into the United States; "Terror Babies" screamed the graphic for the recurring segment (Huffington Post 2011). Instead of "Keeping 'em Honest," as Anderson Cooper calls one of his segments, cable TV is giving voice to people whose letter to the editor wouldn't have been published a decade ago.

Compounding the problem is the growing absence of institutional memory. As the *New York Times* reported in late summer 2011, the "Boys on the Bus"—the title of Timothy Crouse's iconic account of the 1968 presidential campaign press corps—have morphed into the "Kids on the Bus" as news organizations replace veteran political reporters with young reporters just out of school—because they're cheaper (Peters 2011). Where once journalists like Roger Mudd and R.W. Apple provided a nuanced and multidimensional take on politics and policy, today "The best political team on television," as CNN calls its election analysis team, is a bunch of campaign operatives who compete to see whose version of spin sticks with the viewers. And it's only recently that CNN and the other networks bothered to tell us that their so-called experts—on politics, international affairs, and a host of other issues—were also on someone else's payroll and had a large axe to grind.

Media fragmentation has, by no means, killed political reporting. A cottage industry of specialist websites has cropped up providing a blow-by-blow, minute-by-minute, play-by-play from the political battleground. Sites like Politico and PolitiFact.org provide a depth of coverage rarely seen elsewhere. But many of these boutique outfits also benefit from funding from sources that often have their own agendas.

Google's chief executive, Eric Schmidt, once observed that the internet has the potential to become "a cesspool" of false information (Ives 2008). A quick Google search for the keyword "politics" makes it evident truer words were never spoken. Yet survey after survey underlines the reality that many Americans are unable to distinguish between opinion and reportage, between a reputable news organization and a cut-rate blog.

"The basis of our governments being the opinion of the people, the very first object should be to keep that right," Thomas Jefferson wrote more than two centuries ago. "And were it left to me to decide whether we should have a government without newspapers or newspapers without a government, I should not hesitate to prefer the latter" (Kurland and Lerner 1986).

The authors of the essays in the following pages would probably agree. So would those Egyptians I mentioned earlier. People in that country had lived for decades under an authoritarian government without an independent press. Suddenly they found themselves with a newly independent press and no government. And there was dancing in the streets.

References

Huffington Post. 2011. "Anderson Cooper Stuns GOP Rep. on 'Terror Babies.'" May 25. huffingtonpost.com/2010/08/11/anderson-cooper-stuns-gop_n_678650.html.

Ives, Nat. 2008. "Google's Schmidt Says Internet 'Cesspool' Needs Brands." *Ad Age Media News*, October 8. adage.com/article/media/google-s-schmidt-internet-cesspool-brands/131569.

Kurland, Philip B., and Ralph Lerner, eds. 1986. *The Founders' Constitution*, Amendment I (Speech and Press), Document 8, Thomas Jefferson to Edward Carrington, January 16, 1787. Papers 11:48-49. press-pubs.uchicago.edu/founders/documents/amendI_speechs8.html.

Peters, Jeremy W. 2011. "Covering 2012, Youths on the Bus." *New York Times*, August 30. nytimes.com/2011/08/31/business/media/campaign-reporters-are-younger-and-cheaper.html?_r=2&pagewanted=all.

Preston, Peter. 2007. "Reporters Are Always the Key." *The Observer* (London), December 1. guardian.co.uk/business/2007/dec/02/pressandpublishing.comment.

"Remembering Agnew." 1996. Interview by Jim Lehrer, *NewsHour with Jim Lehrer*, PBS, September 18. pbs.org/newshour/bb/remember/agnew_9-18.html.

We Are Guests in Our Readers' Homes

Peter Bhatia, *The Oregonian*

T he idea that we are guests in our readers' homes is a philosophy that still makes sense today for newspapers and journalists. Even in this rapidly and remarkably changing digital media world, it serves us well to remember that the paper gets taken into each subscriber's home every day. It is why maintaining a civil approach to how we present the news still matters. It is why holding strongly to our traditional values of fairness and completeness in our reporting is as essential as ever. And it is why it is important that there must continue to be a healthy respect for reporting all possible views in a story—even at a time when so many have lost the ability to respect the views of others.

Some of this may seem quaint, particularly in the wake of the vigorous and wide-ranging conversation on communication and media that took place at the Civility and Democracy in America conference in Spokane. But with all the noise swirling around the media world today, especially on the Internet, the need has never been greater for an old-fashioned approach, where information is vetted, thoughtful discussion is valued, and adult behavior is the norm. It's called the newspaper.

There needs to be an ongoing counter to the endless partisan arguments on cable TV and the political polarization that dominates the Internet. Newsrooms would be wise to openly position themselves as a place in print and digitally where civil discussion can take place, a wide array of opinions are available (especially in combination with websites), and the political middle still has a home.

How can newsrooms accomplish that? One simple way is to hold the line against the crass language that has become so normal of late. It may be a little thing, but keeping the language in print at a civil level (no obscenities, etc.) is not a bad place to start. Most newspapers are still holding the line, even if the bar online is lower.

Newspapers would also do well to stay focused on what matters. Someone asked recently whether all the silliness on the Internet (Charlie Sheen, etc.) was putting pressure on us to go more that direction with the presentation of news. The answer is perhaps, but such matters are best relegated to the people column and let us keep our covers focused on news.

But the bigger issues still revolve around our journalistic priorities and how we execute that coverage, especially in a time of diminished staff. It is never too late to address the inherent weaknesses in our traditional models of reporting. Political reporting, just to pick one topic, has long moved away from the horserace model and more to issues reporting, but in the end it always seems to come down to polling and who makes the more outrageous statement.

Let us not be afraid to challenge everything we do. We are already doing that in adapting to the digital world. Reporters now shoot video; newspapers aggregate all sorts of local content from myriad sources mainstream and otherwise for their websites. We can help if we further pull our reporting back from the edges and to the middle. It is also time to really allow more diverse views to be aired in our newsrooms and to tie our coverage to a broader set of values than the traditional middle-class majority views that newsroom cultures help endure. This is likely more difficult than ever. As Dietram Scheufele notes in this volume, we surround ourselves with people like us, and in an era of social media where we select our friends, it is more difficult to reach disparate audiences. He wasn't speaking about newsrooms, but he could have been.

Newspapers are not without faults. As was observed in the discussion at the conference, we are still much too prone to the conflict model of reporting. One side says this; the other says that. We too easily gravitate to the extreme views, leaving the vast middle, where most readers reside, uncovered. As Theodore Glasser notes, also in this volume, we are dutiful about reporting the debate, but afraid to instigate the debate for fear of being charged with bias. We have allowed the notion of objectivity to all too often result in bland back-and-forth journalism that stops short of finding the truth. We have let others fill voids in our coverage, at least in part contributing to the polarizing nature of politics in our society today and the rise of talking (and yelling) heads on TV and radio from the right and the left.

It may seem ironic for a newspaper editor whose affiliated website allows anonymous comments to be arguing for civility. The Internet world is still something of a Wild West and the often vulgar and demeaning commentary is hardly a reflection of a civil society. If a story mentions immigration, the bigots come out in droves. Write anything perceived as negative about the University of Oregon football team and the comments turn personal and ugly in an instant. This is a conundrum for newsrooms. Some have required commenters to use their real names. Not surprisingly, their web traffic—and the web is all about traffic—drops dramatically. This remains a work in progress and one that remains unsolved. Free speech and civility do come into conflict. The view from here is that the First Amendment triumphs. But there is much more to be discussed.

In the meantime, we in media sort through this amazing transition where print is still the primary source of our revenue, but digital is the future. It will go on for some time. As that plays out, the hope is that traditional media can remain a refuge for effective and useful civic discourse, regardless of the platform to which we deliver our journalism. We really have nothing to lose by positioning ourselves as a place of sanity. As fellow contributor Russell Dalton wryly observes: We live in a time where statesmen act like comedians and comedians (Jon Stewart) act like statesmen.

Civility, Democracy, and the Mass Media

Russell J. Dalton, University of California, Irvine

IIIIIIIIIIIIIIIIIIIIIIIIIIIIIIIIIIIIIIIIIIIIIIIIIIIIIIIIIIIIIIIIIIIIIIIIIIIIIIIIIIIIIIIIIIIIIIIIIIIIIIIIIIIIIIIIIIIIIIIIIIIIIIIIIIIIIIIIIIIIIIIIIIIIIIII

At the heart of the Spokane symposium lies a belief in the link between civility and both democratic deliberation and decision making. Intolerance, hyperpolarized politics, and personal attacks on partisan opponents erode the very values upon which democracy is based. These actions often come from both the extreme left and extreme right. In most cases such behavior makes it more difficult to have democratic deliberation, an understanding of contrasting viewpoints, and political compromise.

There can be and should be intense political disagreements between political groups in a democracy; such disagreements are part of contemporary American politics. Sometimes contentious politics is necessary, but not as a regular diet. The logic of democracy is to provide a way to peaceably and reasonably resolve political disagreements, while vilifying one's opponents is likely to undermine a deliberative decision making process. As Manent wrote in describing Tocqueville's study of *Democracy in America*, "to love democracy, it is necessary to love it moderately" (1996, 148).

My goal in this essay is to discuss how the media may be contributing to the apparent growth in incivility, and how citizens perceive the media. As the essays in this section illustrate, the media are often viewed as fanning the flames of excess. Probably most discussions of the media begin by highlighting their failings. They are like Roger Dangerfield in that they get little respect. But I think that many of these criticisms are deserved. The media have contributed to the present imagery of American politics, and this may continue or worsen. We should begin by diagnosing the current situation.

Who is Polarized?

Part of the explanation for the apparent decline in political civility is the supposed polarization of America. As famously portrayed on electoral maps on the TV networks, we are divided into red and blue states, red and blue communities, and red and blue citizens. Moreover, these descriptions of the two Americas often take on a pejorative imagery. Some analysts thus see intense divisions in public preferences as the root source of incivility (Bishop 2009, Frank 2004). James Q. Wilson (2006) cites Dave Berry to describe this common bipolar image of the American public:

> residents of Red states are 'ignorant racist fascist knuckle-dragging NASCAR-obsessed cousin-marrying road-kill-eating tobacco-juice-dribbling gun-fondling religious fanatic rednecks,' while Blue-state residents are 'godless unpatriotic pierced-nose Volvo-driving France-loving leftwing Communist latte-sucking tofu-chomping holistic-wacko neurotic vegan weenie perverts.'

There is an intense debate over the topic of polarization in political science (e.g. Abramowitz 2010; Fiorina 2004; Kaufman, Petrocik, and Shaw 2008; Levendusky 2009). In his book *Culture Wars? The Myth of a Polarized America*, Morris Fiorina marshals an impressive mass of data to show that these images are starkly overdrawn. Most Americans have centrist views even on many of the hot button issues of the day. For example, the average citizen does not favor balancing the budget entirely with tax increases or entirely with spending cuts, but with a mix of both. Most Americans do not favor unlimited abortion as advocated by some pro choice groups, and they do not favor entirely restricting abortion as proposed by some pro life groups—most people favor abortion with some conditions. The modal American describes their views as "middle-of-the-road" and not as extremely liberal or conservative.

Furthermore, other public opinion surveys point to the steady growth of political tolerance within the American public (Dalton 2008, 2009). Even though there are continuing challenges in dealing with America's racial and ethnic diversity, tolerance of others has increased dramatically in the past few decades. The recent study *American Grace* demonstrated a breadth of religious tolerance that sharply contradicts the image of a nation engaged in culture wars (Putnam and Campbell 2010). Americans are more tolerant toward a range of political and social groups that would have been stigmatized a generation ago.

In sum, the public at-large is not the primary source of political polarization in America and the incivility that might result from such polarization. Indeed, there are some individuals and small groups of citizens who are uncivil and politically intolerant. But most Americans are centrists and more accepting of others, even those who differ socially or politically. What then is the source of these perceptions of widespread polarization and incivility?

Media Framing

Fiorina offers two primary explanations for the image of America as a deeply divided nation. The first is that political elites and political activists are more divided than the citizenry. Indeed, studies of congressional voting patterns document a steady increase in party polarization over the past few decades. While there was once significant overlap between conservative Democrats and liberal Republicans, the congressional parties have now become more ideologically homogeneous. If anything, the 2010 elections increased this elite polarization. This has lead to frequent concerns about the lack of civility and comity within Congress, and the fading of an era when politicians respected one another even when they disagreed (Fiorina 2004).

Fiorina's second explanation focuses on the media's role in framing political discourse, especially the role of television (21-25). A fair and honest reporting of politics inside the Washington beltway would describe the increasing division and derision that characterizes politics in the capital. The problem, I believe, arises because of how the media decide to frame competition between the two major parties. In search of the grand narrative and compelling stories, media reporting often focuses on examples of individuals who highlight the political extremes rather than the modal citizen. The conservative town in Kansas is compared to a liberal suburb of Boston; or Joe the Plumber is presented as a typical John McCain voter, while a glitzy Hollywood celebrity (or working class African-American) symbolizes Barack Obama voters. This is more engaging television than saying that most voters have positions more moderate than either McCain or Obama.

Another widely noted issue is the development of cable news channels and the 24/7 news cycle.[1] The introduction of Fox News created a different dynamic in television news competition. Rupert Murdoch correctly recognized that many conservative Americans wanted a news source that supported their political views, and Fox News was the result. In reaction, MSNBC morphed into the alternative to Fox by presenting a much more liberal slant on the news. Although ideologues on both sides might disagree, such diversity in news offerings is probably a positive thing for democracy. I am not sure what channel Thomas Jefferson would watch if he were alive today, but he would probably agree that an active public discourse is the way to best address the issues facing a democracy.

However, the prominence given both Fox and MSNBC reinforces the imagery that America is deeply divided between these two alternatives, even though the viewership of both combined represents only a small fraction of eligible voters. More worrisome, however, is the tone of news reporting that has accompanied the fragmentation of the electronic media. Fox's model includes a focus on personalities who present a hyperpolarized view of American conservatives packaged as infotainment. Similarly, MSNBC countered with Keith Olbermann, who described his political opponents as the "worst [people] in the world."

Indeed, this logic of point/counterpoint programming has become so common that I often hear politicians who I consider moderates complain that talk show producers are upset when they do not follow a straight party line. In one memorable recent quote, a talk show guest was told "cut the bipartisan crap and just give us some red meat" (McKinnon 2010). Fox presents a one-dimensional view from the right, MSNBC presents a one-dimensional view from the left, and CNN presents two talking heads, one from each extreme. Where is the center in American politics?

Often, the media's response to these criticisms is to claim that they are simply giving the public what they want. This criticism, it is argued, is like those who suggest people are tired of crime and celebrity exposes on television, but then ratings increase when there is an especially dramatic crime or celebrity scandal.

There is an element of truth to this claim, but we should not accept it whole cloth. First, the most notable examples of ideologically extreme media coverage have relatively low and declining viewership. At his peak in 2009, Glenn Beck drew nearly 3 million viewers a day, but this is less than 2 percent of those who voted in the 2008 election. By 2011, perhaps as a rejection of extremist politics, Beck's ratings had dropped by half. Bill O'Reilly, Rush Limbaugh, and Sean Hannity are also experiencing a declining fan base (Avlon 2011). Before liberals celebrate the death of conservative talk shows, ratings data also documented a steady decline in Keith Olbermann's viewership through 2009-10 until he and MSNBC parted company. At his peak, Olbermann's program drew barely a million viewers a night. Similarly, AirAmerica did not find the listener base to sustain their progressive radio network. These examples suggest that there is a modest viewer base for hyperpolarized media coverage.[2]

Second, there are alternative models. For instance, Jon Stewart's *The Daily Show* has a distinctly liberal audience. The guests on the show range across the political spectrum, and they are greeted by civil, albeit lively conversation. Part of Stewart's appeal is his authenticity; he points out the inconsistency of politicians of both parties—he is an equal opportunity critic. Moreover, Stewart openly speaks for civility in political discourse, and in 2010 sponsored a large "Restore Sanity" rally on the Washington Mall to reinforce the point that Americans are not painted red or blue at birth. This is infotainment without the diatribe (Fox, Koloen, and Sahin 2007; Larris 2005). It is no wonder that young Americans who are disenchanted with political parties and the discourse of political intolerance turn to *The Daily Show* on a regular basis.

My other counter model is to compare the nature of discourse on FOX, MSNBC, or CNN to the discourse on ESPN. Sports are a real competition, between football players trying to physically overwhelm their opponents or hockey players engaging in fisticuffs. But the culture of sports reporting is to be civil and unbiased. Even the combatants typically have civil words for their opponents before and after the competition. ESPN analysts typically analyze, rather than specialize in bombast and uncivil discussion. Even as a political science professor, I often become frustrated and aggravated by the hyperpolarized talking heads on CNN; when I do, I turn to ESPN to see sports news without polemics. What does it say about the media in America when ESPN is more civil than the cable news channels?

In summary, the problem is not that the media are diverse in their political views—diverse discussion is good for democracy. The problem is that the choice of frames that the media apply to political discourse is adversarial by design and amplifies the debates among party elites who are very polarized. It pictures Americans as having a choice between extreme positions, often couched in uncivil descriptions of the other, while downplaying the modest views of the American public as a whole.

Popular Reactions to the Media

In addition to declining viewership, another sign of the current problem is the public's growing cynicism about the media. Since the mid-1970s the General Social Survey has asked Americans about public confidence in various social and political institutions. When this question was first asked in 1973, 85 percent of the public expressed confidence in the press and 78 percent expressed confidence in television news.[3] But these opinions trended downward over the next several decades (Figure 1). By the most recent survey in 2008, little more than half the public said they were confident about either medium. The Gallup Poll (2011) displays a similar long-term decline in the percent believing the media are reporting the news fully, accurately, and fairly. This dropped from 68 percent positive in 1972 to only 44 percent in 2011.

The Pew Center for People and the Press has surveyed popular images of the media in more detail. A 2011 report warned that the media's image had hit a two decade low (Pew Research Center 2011). In 1985, only 34 percent of Americans thought news organizations often had inaccurate stories; this grew to 66 percent by 2011. Feelings that the press is politically biased rose from 45 percent to 60 percent over the same timespan; doubts about the media's fairness grew from 53 percent of Americans to 77 percent. Almost across the board, the public has become critical of the media's performance.

Figure 1 is the percent expressing "a great deal" or "only some" confidence in each medium (General Social Survey 2010).

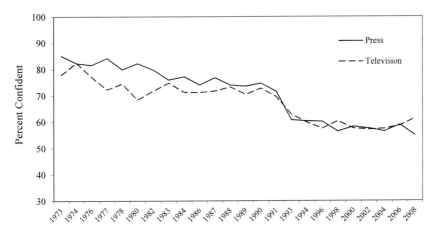

Figure 1. Erosion in Popular Confidence in the Press and Television

This diminished confidence in the media should be upsetting for those who manage the media. It signals that the media's presentation of the news is not what the public wants or expects—in contrast to claims that the media are simply reflecting citizen preferences. And to the extent that a fair and accurate press is essential to meaningful democracy, public skepticism of the media's performance of this role should not be a welcomed development.

What is to be Done?

Social change typically occurs slowly and through diffuse effects, and thus there is not a single answer to how to improve the civility in American politics. A starting point is to recognize the issue and discuss it, as was done at the Spokane symposium, and bring diverse groups of people together to consider options for improving our political discourse. The public education programs that will flow from the symposium are a next step, to reinforce the positive features of the American political culture through continuing political education. As citizens, we can also learn to turn off the bombastic television anchor and be skeptical of those who offer simple answers to the nation's complex problems.

However, the change has to go deeper and be more institutionalized. The culture of Washington politicians and the political parties is eroding the spirit of the nation by preaching incivility, intolerance, and the unwillingness to compromise. Too many people believe we are divided into red and blue citizens with fundamental and irreconcilable differences between us. The media can play a significant role in providing a more accurate view of politics and public preferences because they both reflect and shape the political discourse. One change would be for television programmers and news directors to focus on informed dialogues rather than deaf monologues. When a talk show guest yells at the other guests, a civil mediator response is to ask for reasonable dialogue or turn off the microphone—not to rebook the guest to add more drama to a future telecast. Too much scripted confrontation opens the potential for innovative programming that has liberals and conservatives who bring their values to the table, but who sometimes agree with one another. The desire for drama is understandable because of the nature of the mass media, but not something to encourage through the programming of the news.

Another possible change involves the culture of journalism. One senses that young journalism students are growing beyond the 'gotcha' journalism of the post-Watergate era and the ideological excess of some cable news personalities. Some media observers might be alarmed to hear a dean of a leading school of journalism in the Northeast say that his students look to Jon Stewart as a role model of fair and honest reporting. Stewart is on the Comedy Channel after all, and not a regular in the White House press briefings or Sunday talk shows. I believe these sentiments among the young reflect a desire for journalism to develop a longer term perspective on what is important in reporting, and to eschew the strategy of facilitating the hyperpolarization of some politicians (and figures in the mass media). But change will be slow and incomplete. And we will continue to complain about the media—this comes naturally in a democracy.

Notes

1. I do not discuss Internet news sources, but these are an important new source of political information. For young Americans the Internet now exceeds both television and newspapers as an information source, and is the only medium that has gained audience size since 2008. The anonymity and diffuse nature of the Internet also changes the nature of discourse and perhaps invites incivility in some forums.
2. Viewership of all news programs on the three major broadcast and cable networks decreased since 2008, as Internet usage increased as an information source. But even if the hyperpartisan news programs retained their base viewers, these still represent a small share of the American electorate (Pew Research Center 2011).
3. Even these levels were modest, because confident includes about a sixth who express "a great deal" of confidence and more than half the public said "only some" confidence (General Social Survey 2010).

References

Abramowitz, Alan. 2010. *The Disappearing Center: Engaged Citizens, Polarization, and American Democracy*. New Haven: Yale University Press.

Avlon, John. 2011. "Is Right-Wing Talk Dying?" *Daily Beast*, February 9. thedailybeast.com/articles/2011/02/09/glenn-beck-sean-hannity-ratings-drop-right-wing-talk-is-dying.html.

Bishop, Bill. 2009. *The Big Sort: Why the Clustering of Like-Minded America is Tearing Us Apart*. New York: Mariner Books.

Dalton, Russell. 2008. *Citizen Politics: Public Opinion and Political Parties in Advanced Industrial Democracies*. Washington, DC: CQ Press, ch. 6.

_____. 2009. *The Good Citizen: How a Younger Generation is Reshaping American Politics*, rev. ed. Washington, DC: CQ Press, ch. 5.

Fiorina, Morris P. 2004. *Culture War? The Myth of a Polarized America*. With Samuel J. Abrams and Jeremy C. Pope. New York: Pearson, Longman.

Fox, Julia R., Glory Koloen, and Volkan Sahin. 2007. "No Joke: A Comparison of Substance in *The Daily Show with Jon Stewart* and Broadcast Network Television Coverage of the 2004 Presidential Election Campaign." *Journal of Broadcasting and Electronic Media* 51(2): 213-227.

Frank, Thomas. 2004. *What's the Matter with Kansas? How Conservatives Won the Heart of America*. New York: Metropolitan Books.

Gallup. 2011. "Media Use and Evaluation." gallup.com/poll/1663/Media-Use-Evaluation.aspx.

General Social Survey. 2010. norc.uchicago.edu/GSS+Website.

Kaufman, Karen M., John R. Petrocik, and Daron R. Shaw. 2008. *Unconventional Wisdom: Facts and Myths about American Voters*. New York: Oxford University Press, ch. 3.

Larris, Rachel Joy. 2005. "The *Daily Show* Effect: Humor, News, Knowledge and Viewers." Unpublished masters thesis, Georgetown University.

Levendusky, Matthew. 2009. *The Partisan Sort: How Liberals Became Democrats and Conservatives Became Republicans*. Chicago: University of Chicago Press.

Manent, Pierre. 1996. *Tocqueville and the Nature of Democracy*. Lanham, MD: Rowman and Littlefield.

McKinnon, Mark. 2010. Comments on CNN's *Reliable Sources*. November 14. transcripts.cnn.com/TRANSCRIPTS/1011/14/rs.01.html.

Pew Research Center. 2011. "Press Widely Criticized, But Trusted More than Other Information Sources." Center for the People and the Press, September 22. people-press.org/2011/09/22/press-widely-criticized-but-trusted-more-than-other-institutions.

_____. 2011. *State of the News Media 2011*. Project for Excellence in Journalism. stateofthemedia.org.

Putnam, Robert D., and David E. Campbell. 2010. *American Grace: How Religion Divides and Unites Us*. New York: Simon and Schuster.

Wilson, James Q. 2006. "How Divided Are We?" *Commentary* 121(2): 15-21.

News, Inclusion, and the Challenge of Civility

Theodore L. Glasser, Stanford University

ow should we respond when in principle civility presupposes inclusion but when in practice it favors exclusion? What does it mean to promote civility when civility itself becomes a coercive force—when in effect, if not by design, its claims serve to exclude speakers and their speech? Basically, what do we do when pleas for civility constrict rather than enlarge the opportunities for public discussion and debate?

In these few pages I'd like to explore these questions in the context of American democracy and especially American journalism. I'd like to make the case—more provocatively than conclusively—that certain practices in American journalism, rooted in certain presuppositions about American democracy and more broadly American culture, limit and narrow public discourse. Specifically, I want to look at news as a form of public discourse, focusing on how civility in journalism, understood as a set of enduring claims about proper and acceptable communication, constrains in occasionally pernicious ways the press's ability to accommodate a full range of voices and perspectives.

Indeed, the prospects for a public discourse that disenfranchises large numbers of citizens, especially citizens associated with minority interests and perspectives, prompts Iris Marion Young to take seriously an often neglected feature of democratic participation: communication. Young embraces the basic premise of deliberative, as opposed to interest-based, theories of democracy, but moves beyond that by considering a question that political theorists seldom ask: "What are the norms and conditions of inclusive democratic communication under circumstances of structural inequality and cultural difference?" (Young 2006, 6). Of obvious relevance to journalism and its roles and responsibilities in multicultural societies, Young's question underscores the importance of accommodating what she describes as "differently situated knowledge," which requires, she argues, "an equal privileging of any forms of communicative interaction where people aim to reach understanding" (Young 1996, 128, 125).

Young's idea of a "communicative democracy," understood roughly as an approach to deliberation that ties differences in communication (form and content alike) to differences in social position rather than differences in identity—a subtle but significant shift from a politics of identity to a politics of difference—provides a foundation and serves as a point of departure for a quick examination of two related but broadly distinguishable issues concerning our expectations for civility in journalism. The first concerns the presumption of deliberation, when we risk confusing models of democracy we wish applied to journalism with models of democracy that actually account for press practices and performance, which not only creates a yawning gap between journalism and its critics but renders journalism's critics ineffectual in their calls for a broader and arguably better conception of civility. The second concerns the domestication of diversity in journalism, which has the effect of discounting the very "differently situated knowledge" that Young would expect journalists to factor into their reporting and writing. I conclude with a few paragraphs devoted to the prospects for civility in journalism if we can open up journalism by putting new, more, and different people in control of it.

Democracy and the Politics of Diversity

Given all the "d" words associated with the ideal of democratic participation and popular sovereignty, a vocabulary especially popular among academics and civic leaders—discourse, discussion, dialogue, debate, deliberation—it's easy to forget that these terms, alone or in combination, serve poorly as descriptions of democracy as most Americans experience it. The same is true for journalism and journalists. The American press, like the American electorate, understands democratic participation in terms of competition, conflict, autonomy, freedom of choice, personal liberty, individual initiative—precisely the vocabulary that characterizes the interest-based theory of democracy that Young and other deliberative theorists reject. Notwithstanding the occasional call to reform journalism and thereby reform democracy—the "public journalism" movement of the 1990s is a good example (see e.g. Glasser 1999, Haas 2007)—journalism in the United States remains wedded to a view of democracy in which a commitment to civility can easily mask a disregard for differences in social position and social perspective, the result of which is the exclusion of speakers whose interests seem unreasonable and/or whose speech violates the prevailing norms of acceptable discourse.

One useful way to appreciate the depth and consequences of the divide between journalism's democratic assumptions and the democratic assumptions that inform so many of journalism's critics is to look at the essential differences between, to employ an intentionally overdrawn distinction, "pluralism" and "multiculturalism." To recycle an argument developed in greater detail elsewhere (Glasser, Awad, and Kim 2009, 57-78), pluralism and multiculturalism represent contrasting approaches to the relationship between democracy and cultural diversity. Pluralism denotes a view of democracy in which individuals, acting alone or in cooperation with others, secure the resources and influence they need to pursue their interests and satisfy their desires. Pluralists view politics as a more or less private contest—a competition—between private parties and their private interests; they defer to the logic of market forces, which they take to be "natural" and thus unbiased, for a just resolution of differences and disagreements. Multiculturalism, in contrast, begins with the proposition, to use Michael Sandel's version of it, that "we can know a good in common that we cannot know alone" (1982, 183). Multiculturalists regard politics as a conspicuously public activity aimed at the discovery of shared or common interests which may or may not coincide with any individual's personal or private interests; they reject pluralism's faith in the inherent fairness and impartiality of the marketplace and turn instead to venues for political participation that facilitate debate and discussion and which, with few exceptions, require an equitable distribution of resources.

As a theory of democracy developed in the decades following World War II, pluralism—otherwise known as "liberal pluralism," "interest-group democracy," or "empirical democratic theory"—offers a fundamentally descriptive and therefore conservative account of Western democracy. Fueled by the apparent success of democracies in the United States, Britain, and elsewhere, pluralism celebrates what it takes to be a broad and enduring political consensus—"a consensus on the rules of procedure; a consensus on the range of policy options; a consensus on the legitimate scope of political activity" (Held 1987, 194)—and the legitimacy it confers on existing institutions and arrangements. Thus, given pluralism's overall satisfaction with the status quo, political change usually amounts to small fixes and minor repairs. As one of pluralism's chief theoreticians, Robert Dahl, once put it, democracies in the pluralist tradition envision a political culture "that brings about reform more through mutual adjustment and gradual accumulation of incremental changes than through sweeping programs of comprehensive and coordinated reconstruction" (1967, 190).

More overtly normative in its claims and outlook, multiculturalism tries to address rather than bracket patterns of social inequality. From the perspective of multiculturalism, politics exists in history, not in nature; and history provides ample evidence, as Seyla Benhabib reminds us, of "relations of oppression, domination, exploitation, and denigration" (1999, 404). To be sure, multiculturalism regards as essentially undemocratic any approach to politics that views individual initiative as a realistic remedy for individuals who find themselves lodged in a disadvantaged social position. What matters to multiculturalists, but not to pluralists, is the *capacity* of individuals to participate in the processes through which their interests can be made known and rendered acceptable to others. In short, pluralists ascribe equality; multiculturalists work to achieve it.

Cultural Diversity and Democratic Participation

Pluralism's ascription of equality manifests itself as a pledge to promote what in the context of race is often called a "color-blind" society. This means that minority groups become yet another interest group, treated without regard for differences in power or privilege. Put a little differently, individuals and groups of individuals in a pluralist society can advance their "private" interests but they cannot, given pluralism's celebrated consensus, claim a "public" interest in altering the conditions for political participation. Paradoxically, citizens in a pluralist society either consent to the consensus that legitimizes a pluralist democracy, even when that consensus works to their disadvantage, or they forfeit their own legitimacy.

Whereas pluralism, then, robs minority groups of whatever substantive claims they might have about their rights and opportunities to participate in the larger society, multiculturalism offers an account of culture and cultural groups that equates political parity with political participation. Multiculturalism promotes deliberation, not competition, by creating a space—what Jürgen Habermas famously calls a "public sphere"—that "obeys not the structure of market processes but the obstinate structure of public communication oriented to mutual understanding" (1996, 23). In this space—or spaces, to acknowledge the likelihood of a multiplicity of public spheres—individuals and groups of individuals dedicate themselves to an equal consideration of the interests of everyone, which is to say that a multicultural society invites everyone to consider the plight of everyone else. Under the norms of multiculturalism, it follows, individuals do not merely express their interests but transform them: "Through the process of public discussion," Young writes, "people often gain new information, learn of different experiences of their collective problems, or find that their own initial opinions are founded on prejudice or ignorance, or that they have misunderstood the relation of their own interests to others" (2000, 26). Bound by the regulative ideal of reciprocity, which Young defines as an acknowledgement "that the interests of others must be taken into account in order to reach a judgment" (30), individuals do not merely tolerate different interests but work together to find mutually agreeable interpretations of them. Through their commitment to open and accessible discussions, individuals come to value the right to be heard as an opportunity to be understood. (For a useful and relevant discussion of the opportunity to be understood, see Husband 1998.)

The opportunity to be understood, which builds on but extends considerably beyond the right to be heard and the right to hear, highlights the importance of what Young calls a "relational" view of culture. Mindful of the essentialist logic that reduces cultural groups to "a set of common attributes that all of their members share," Young focuses on the "experience, history and social knowledge" that provide "a general orientation to political issues" (2000, 136, 148). These *social* perspectives come from shared positions in society, not from what might seem to be the "essential" features of the people who inhabit those positions. To be precise, social *perspectives* do "not contain a determinate specific content," Young explains, but consist "in a set of questions, kinds of experiences, and assumptions with which reasoning begins, rather than conclusions drawn" (137). Thus, the nexus between a relational view of culture and the opportunity to be understood rests not on an appreciation or even an awareness of the intricacies of different cultures per se but on a recognition that cultural differences can—and often do—correspond to the sometimes very different ways in which individuals know and experience the world in which they live.

Journalism and the Future of Civility

Accounts of these differences—that is, accounts of the differences in the way people live and understand their lives—seldom end up in the mainstream American press, at least not in any politically meaningful sense. Journalists will, of course, cover the interests of individuals and groups of individuals, including, increasingly, the interests of minorities of all kinds, but that coverage typically looks past differences in social perspective and concentrates instead on interests that can be reasonably framed as being in legitimate competition with other interests. True to the spirit of pluralism, most

American newsrooms shy away from coverage of interests—and disregard entirely the perspectives associated with them—whenever interests convey, even subtly, a disdain for the consensus that establishes, among other norms, the boundaries for civil discourse.

A good illustration of this tendency toward exclusion comes from a recent comparison of mainstream and minority media in their coverage of a local issue—the proposed redevelopment of a neighborhood shopping center—of particular interest to the Latina/o community in San Jose, California (Glasser, Awad, and Kim 2009, 63-75). The mainstream press—a chain-owned daily and a weekly Spanish-language newspaper owned and operated by it—covered the issue as a clash of interests made newsworthy by a related event: a meeting, an announcement, a protest, a lawsuit. Coverage was characteristically fair and balanced, providing ample opportunity for city officials and the redevelopment firm to express their support for a new shopping center and for local shopkeepers and shop owners to express their disapproval. Disengaged and dispassionate, reporters from the mainstream press wrote about the controversy from the vantage point of a disinterested bystander.

The minority press—two locally owned and operated Latina/o newspapers—covered the issue very differently, often without any reference to an event. Most of the coverage portrayed the shopping center controversy as one more example of the indignities and injustice San Jose's Latina/o community had endured for decades. Hardly disengaged and dispassionate, reporters wrote from the perspective of *their* community and the struggle of *their* people. Although reasonably fair in soliciting and publishing quotes from city officials and others who supported the redevelopment plan, the minority papers positioned their reporters as compatriots whose ties to the community strengthened, rather than weakened, their credibility as journalists. These reporters understood first-hand, and their stories conveyed, what was for them the real issue: a history of neglect, indifference, discrimination, and poverty.

Because the disinterested journalism of the mainstream press rests on the pluralist premise of a generally acceptable social and political order, it treats competing interests as a conflict within, not as challenge to, the status quo. In this case, nothing in the mainstream press hinted at problems with the prevailing patterns of power in San Jose. For the minority press, however, coverage of this kind serves as an act of resistance. Readers needed to be informed, obviously, but they also needed to be alerted to—and mobilized against—yet another instance of the City of San Jose's disregard for its disenfranchised Latino/a community. For the owners and staff of the two minority newspapers, the point of their coverage was not simply to get their readers added to the roster of players in the game of politics, though that was important; they also wanted to change the rules of the game.

But, alas, if as a general proposition the mainstream press conserves the status quo and the minority press challenges it, do we not then have the kind of diversity of journalism that a multicultural society needs? No, and for three reasons. First, American journalism lacks a coherent infrastructure. Notwithstanding new plans for partnerships and collaboration, many of them driven by the decline in size and number of American daily newspapers, most newsrooms view other newsrooms as competitors, a convention of American journalism that diminishes the opportunities for the cooperation and coordination that would create needed relationships between mainstream and minority journalism. Too many minority media function as enclaves, isolated and removed from the larger media landscape and thus unable to serve as points of entry to successively larger debates and discussion. This is why Young views "linkage" as a "necessary condition for political communication" (2006, 53). In whatever form they might take, linkages imply a planned and intentional relationship between and among newsrooms, a relationship intended to cultivate and amplify minority voices.

Second, the apparent abundance of minority media in the United States is misleading. Many minority media are minority in name only, a designation at times applied to any newsroom that produces material in a language other than English. Many of these media cater to a niche market, not a discernible community, and do so with little or no regard for their audience's social position and social perspective. Where minority media are needed most—in poor and neglected neighborhoods—they are least likely to exist. As difficult as it may be to challenge the hegemony of the journalism-as-a-business model, which equates a free press with free enterprise, the future of minority journalism is likely to depend on new institutional arrangements and a structurally mixed system of public communication that can accommodate forms of journalism beyond what markets can sustain.

Third, as tempting as it may be to turn to technology for answers to questions about the future of inclusivity in journalism, the recent and rapid computerization of communication has not yet delivered on its promise to diversify and democratize American journalism. Mainstream newsrooms, particularly the newsrooms of metropolitan daily newspapers, still account for most of the original news content produced in the United States; ultimately, if not always directly, most Americans get most of their news from the same few sources. And then there is the more basic question of access to technology. In the case of California's Latino/a population, for example, 35 percent of adults never use the Internet; and only 50 percent have broadband access at home (James 2011).

For American democracy and particularly American journalism, the future of civility depends on finding ways to include in the day's debates and discussions the voices of subordinated groups whose interests cannot be accommodated within, and must thus be viewed as a challenge to, the prevailing political consensus. This means making room for truly radical claims—radical in the sense of the Latin *radix*, going to the roots of the situation. More than that, a commitment to civility implies an openness to a full spectrum of forms of expression, so that unpopular or unfamiliar standards of "articulateness" do not become grounds for exclusion. "None of us," as Young puts it, "should be excluded or marginalized in situations of political discussion because we fail to express ourselves according to culturally specific norms of tone, grammar, and diction" (2000, 39). Finally, the prospects for civility in journalism, like the prospects for civility elsewhere in society, require a rejection of conceptions of competition that diminish the value of a group's perspective or inhibit the cooperation, coordination, and collaboration needed to cultivate and circulate a group's expression of interests.

References

Benhabib, Seyla. 1999. "The Liberal Imagination and the Four Dogmas of Multiculturalism." *Yale Journal of Criticism* 12(2): 401-413.

Dahl, Robert A. 1967. *Pluralist Democracy in the United States: Conflict and Consent*. Chicago: Rand McNally.

Glasser, Theodore L., ed. 1999. *The Idea of Public Journalism*. New York: Guilford.

Glasser, Theodore L., Isabel Awad and John W. Kim. 2009. "The Claims of Multiculturalism and Journalism's Promise of Diversity." *Journal of Communication* 59(1): 57-78.

Haas, Tanni. 2007. *The Pursuit of Public Journalism: Theory, Practice, and Criticism*. New York: Routledge.

Habermas, Jürgen. 1996. "Three Normative Models of Democracy." In *Democracy and Difference: Contesting the Boundaries of the Political*, edited by Seyla Benhabib. Princeton, NJ: Princeton University Press.

Held, David. 1987. *Models of Democracy*. Stanford, CA: Stanford University Press.

Husband, Charles. 1998. "Differentiated Citizenship and the Multi-ethnic Public Sphere." *Journal of International Communication* 5(1&2): 134-148.

James, Scott. 2011. "Hispanics Rank High On Digital Divide." *The New York Times*, June 17, A29.

Sandel, Michael 1982. *Liberalism and the Limits of Justice*. New York: Cambridge University Press.

Young, Iris Marion. 1996. "Communication and the Other: Beyond Deliberative Democracy."
    In *Democracy and Difference: Contesting the Boundaries of the Political*, edited by Seyla
    Benhabib, 120-136. Princeton, NJ: Princeton University Press.
_____. 2000. *Inclusion and Democracy*. New York: Oxford University Press.
_____. 2006. "De-centered Deliberative Democracy." *Kettering Review* 24.

The Dangerous Amalgam of Modern Political Discourse

Dietram A. Scheufele, University of Wisconsin-Madison

C ivility in American politics is often treated as a macro-level phenomenon, and much of the academic work on the topic has focused on the nature and tone of our societal discourse more broadly. While some bemoan the decline of civility in that discourse, others have pointed out that in a historical comparison, today's political discourse may in fact be much more civil than it was during various periods in America's past (Schudson 1998).

One aspect that tends to get shorter shrift in academic treatments of civility, however, are the micro-level processes surrounding day-to-day political discussions among citizens. How can civil or uncivil conversations among citizens, for instance, shape their ability and willingness to participate in the political process? And what types of political talk constitute the "soul" of democracy that Tocqueville talked about ([1835-1840] 1969)? Let me outline a few thoughts on both questions, focusing on both the normative aspects and the empirical realities of civil discourse in modern political systems.

The Nature of Political Talk

From a normative perspective, the notion of a truly deliberative (or civil) society is based on a few key premises (Scheufele 2011). Among them are two that are particularly relevant for thinking operationally about civility in day-to-day discussions among citizens: (1) All possible views and supporting arguments are expressed; and (2) participants are willing to listen to and engage with arguments that are different from their own. As a result, civil deliberations among citizens can be defined as the rational exchange of non-likeminded views—or disagreement.

As is so often the case, empirical realities are at odds with these normative ideals. Most attempts to bring citizens together in deliberative settings, such as town hall meetings (DeSantis 1998; DeSantis and Renner 1997) or consensus conferences (Fishkin 1991, 1996) have had very mixed success for a number of related reasons.

(1) Overall participation in these events tends to be low, and many surveys show only about 5 percent of all citizens having participated in public forums or town hall meetings (Scheufele 2011).

(2) Participants in public meetings, even if sampled carefully, differ significantly from the general population, based on demographic, attitudinal, and informational characteristics (Merkle 1996).

(3) Even among those who participate in deliberative meetings, previous research has found significant inequities with respect to how actively they engage in exchanges with other citizens during those meetings (Merkle 1996).

Our Unfamiliarity with Disagreement, and Why It Matters

One of the key explanations for our unwillingness and inability to engage in deliberative exchanges with other citizens is—at least in part—a function of us not being very experienced at it. Many of us are simply not used to being confronted with others on a regular basis who hold views that are diametrically opposed to our own. Our social networks, i.e., the people we are surrounded by in most of our daily activities, tend to be extremely homogenous in their demographic and ideological makeup. We buy houses, socialize, play sports, and discuss politics mostly with people who think and look like us. And as a result, we do not often talk to people that hold different views from our own (Mutz 2002b).

And this may not necessarily be a bad thing. In fact, some researchers have argued that when we do encounter heterogeneity or disagreement in our social networks, it can have detrimental effects on our willingness to engage in the political process. Mutz (2002a), for example, argues that being exposed to non-likeminded political information in one's social network can create feelings of ambivalence among voters and consequently promote apathy rather than engagement with the political process.

And new information environments may make matters worse by allowing us to be even more selective and filter out non-likeminded information from our news diet. This happens at two levels.

At an individual level, news portals and aggregator sites allow for highly effective individual pre-selection of the information that reaches us. iGoogle, myYahoo, and other news aggregators allow us to selectively attend to news items, based on a set of fine-grained filters that can include medium, outlet, content, author, and a host of other search criteria.

This individual-level set of filters, however, is being complemented by possibly even more effective social filters. Seventy-five percent of online news consumers now say they get news forwarded through email or posts on social networking sites (Purcell et al. 2010), i.e., information that is passed along and preselected by people who think just like them. As a result, we may be moving toward a society where we are less and less exposed to (and less and less used to) disagreement and incivility. And that may not be a good thing.

Let me outline why and—in the process—share some empirical data on how all of this plays out during day-to-day exchanges among citizens. In some of our recent work at the University of Wisconsin, my colleagues and I compared citizens whose discussion networks exposed them to disagreement more or less frequently (Kim, Scheufele, and Han, forthcoming; Scheufele et al. 2006; Scheufele et al. 2004). Two of our key questions were: Why does disagreement matter? And what are the effects of people's social environment on their willingness to participate in the political process?

The punch line is consistent across studies: encountering disagreement in one's social network is a good thing. In many cases, it promotes participation and a number of civically-relevant outcomes (McLeod, Scheufele, and Moy 1999; Scheufele et al. 2006; Scheufele et al. 2004).

But some of our most recent studies also showed a significantly stronger positive link between exposure to heterogeneous networks and participation for people who are more likely to express opinions in their exchanges with non-likeminded others than those who do not (Kim, Scheufele, and Han, forthcoming). In other words, disagreement and even incivility in discussions about politics can be a good thing. But it does depend on how willing citizens are to actively participate in these discussions.

Uncivil and Non-Participatory: The Dangerous Amalgam of Modern Political Discourse

Political discussions—in this respect—may be a bit like sports. The payoff from sitting passively in our recliners, holding a can of beer, and watching March Madness is probably minimal. Watching sports on TV does not get us in shape. In fact, it may make us slightly obese and even more apathetic. But actively participating in a team sport is a different story. Going out on the basketball court and playing against another team may leave us bruised and sore the next morning, but—in the long run—it is what keeps us in shape.

The parallels between sports and civil or uncivil exchanges among citizens go even further than that. Similar to watching a basketball game on TV, passive, armchair disagreement does not strengthen our "democratic" muscle. In fact, some research suggests that it may have negative effects, and that exposure to uncivil discourse in talk shows can have detrimental effects on people's trust in various aspects of the political system (Mutz and Reeves 2005).

The positive effects of disagreement and maybe even incivility may therefore come from entering the fray and actively participating in the game, to stay in the basketball analogy. This would certainly be consistent with the significantly stronger positive link between exposure to heterogeneous views and political participation we found for active participants in political discussions than for those who spoke up less (Kim, Scheufele, and Han, forthcoming).

Like many commentators, I continue to be unconvinced that the political climate in the United States is characterized or even threatened by an increasingly uncivil discourse. More importantly, even if there is a trend toward less civility, the tone of public discourse in itself may not be a problem. Instead, many of the studies outlined in this essay point to a slightly more complex diagnosis.

In particular, the United States may have reached a point where our discourse is both uncivil *and* non-participatory. And it is really the combination of both of these characteristics that is the problem, not the lack of civility by itself. Spirited discussions among politically active citizens, even if they are not perfectly civil at times, are a prerequisite of any functioning democracy. A political environment in which chronically apathetic voters see themselves as disconnected observers of hyperpartisan and often uncivil exchanges among pundits and politicians, on the other hand, is equally unhealthy for individual citizens and for the political system more broadly.

References

DeSantis, Victor S. 1998. "Patterns of Citizen Participation in Local Politics: Evidence from New England Town Meetings." Presented at the annual convention of the Midwest Political Science Association. Chicago, IL.

DeSantis, Victor S., and Tari Renner. 1997. "Democratic Traditions in New England Town Meetings: Myths and Realities." Presented at the annual convention of the Midwest Political Science Association. Chicago, IL.

Fishkin, James S. 1991. *Democracy and Deliberation: New Directions for Democratic Reform.* New Haven: Yale University Press.

———. 1996. "Bringing Deliberation to Democracy." *Public Perspective* 7(1): 1-4.

Kim, E., D.A. Scheufele, and J.Y. Han. Forthcoming. "Structure or Predisposition? Exploring the Interaction Effect of Discussion Orientation and Discussion Heterogeneity on Political Participation." *Mass Communication and Society*.

McLeod, Jack M., Dietram A. Scheufele, and Patricia Moy. 1999. "Community, Communication, and Participation: The Role of Mass Media and Interpersonal Discussion in Local Political Participation." *Political Communication* 16(3): 315-336.

Merkle, Daniel M. 1996. "The Polls—Review: The National Issues Convention Deliberative Poll." *Public Opinion Quarterly* 60(4): 588-619.

Mutz, Diana C. 2002a. "The Consequences of Cross-Cutting Networks for Political Participation." *American Journal of Political Science* 46(4): 838-855.

———. 2002b. "Cross-Cutting Social Networks: Testing Democratic Theory in Practice." *American Political Science Review* 96(1): 111-126.

Mutz, Diana C., and Byron Reeves. 2005. "The New Videomalaise: Effects of Televised Incivility on Political Trust." *American Political Science Review* 99(1): 1-15.

Purcell, Kristen, Lee Rainie, Amy Mitchell, Tom Rosenstiel, and Kenny Olmstead. 2010. "Understanding the Participatory News Consumer." *Pew Internet and American Life Project*, March 1. pewinternet.org/Reports/2010/Online-News.aspx.

Scheufele, Dietram A. 2011. "Modern Citizenship or Policy Dead End? Evaluating the Need for Public Participation in Science Policy Making, and Why Public Meetings May Not be the Answer." Joan Shorenstein Center on the Press, Politics and Public Policy. Research Paper Series #R-34. Cambridge, MA: Harvard University. hks.harvard.edu/presspol/publications/papers/research_papers/r34_scheufele.pdf.

Scheufele, Dietram A., Bruce W. Hardy, Dominique Brossard, Israel S. Waismel-Manor, and Erik Nisbet. 2006. "Democracy Based on Difference: Examining the Links between Structural Heterogeneity, Heterogeneity of Discussion Networks, and Democratic Citizenship." *Journal of Communication* 56(4): 728-753.

Scheufele, Dietram A., Matthew C. Nisbet, Dominique Brossard, and Erik C. Nisbet. 2004. "Social Structure and Citizenship: Examining the Impacts of Social Setting, Network Heterogeneity, and Informational Variables on Political Participation." *Political Communication* 21(3): 315-338.

Schudson, Michael. 1998. *The Good Citizen: A History of American Civic Life*. New York: Martin Kessler Books.

Tocqueville, A. (1835-1840) 1969. *Democracy in America*. Garden City, NY: Anchor Books.

Contributors

Peter Bhatia

Peter Bhatia is editor and vice president of the *Oregonian*. He has been in journalism for more than 35 years, working at papers in Spokane, San Francisco, Sacramento, and Dallas. Projects in newsrooms he has helped lead have won seven Pulitzer Prizes (including four in Portland). A Northwest native, he was born and grew up in Pullman, Washington. He is a graduate of Stanford University.

Paul Boyer

Paul Boyer is the Merle Curti Professor of History Emeritus at the University of Wisconsin-Madison. His books include *When Time Shall Be No More: Prophecy Belief in Modern American Culture* (1992) and *Urban Masses and Moral Order in America, 1820–1920* (1978). He is author or coauthor of *The Enduring Vision: A History of the American People* (7th ed., 2010) and *Promises to Keep: The United States Since World War II* (3rd ed., 2004). He edited *The Oxford Companion to United States History* (2001) and *The Oxford Encyclopedia of American History* (12 vols., forthcoming). His essays have appeared in the *New York Times*, *Washington Post Magazine*, the *Nation*, the *New Republic*, the *Chronicle of Higher Education*, and elsewhere.

Thomas Christiano

Thomas Christiano is a professor of philosophy and law at the University of Arizona. He has been a visiting fellow at All Souls College, Oxford. He has been a fellow of the National Humanities Center in Durham, North Carolina, and of the Udall Center for Studies in Public Policy. He is associate editor of *Politics, Philosophy, and Economics* (Sage Publishers). He has published papers and books in the areas of democratic theory, distributive justice, moral philosophy, and political philosophy. He is now engaged in projects on the foundations of equality as a principle of distributive justice and on the basis of international justice, and he is finishing a book entitled *The Constitution of Equality* to be published by Oxford University Press.

Cornell W. Clayton

Cornell W. Clayton is the Claudius O. Johnson Distinguished Professor of Political Science at Washington State University and has been the director of the Thomas S. Foley Institute for Public Policy and Public Service since 2008. His research focuses on American political institutions, law, and judicial politics, and he is currently working on a book titled *The Supreme Court and the Political Regime*, to be published by the University of Chicago Press. Previous books include *Washington State Government and Politics* (WSU Press, 2004), *The Supreme Court in American Politics* (University Press of Kansas, 1999), *Supreme Court Decision-Making* (University of Chicago, 1999), *Government Lawyers* (University Press of Kansas, 1995), and *The Politics of Justice* (M.E. Sharpe, 1992). He currently also serves as the coeditor of *Political Research Quarterly*.

Joshua Cohen

Joshua Cohen is the Marta Sutton Weeks Professor of Ethics in Society and professor of political science, philosophy, and law at Stanford University. A political philosopher, Cohen has written on issues of democratic theory and global justice. He is the author of *Philosophy, Politics, Democracy* (2009), *Rousseau: A Free Community of Equals* (2010), and *The Arc of the Moral Universe and Other Essays* (2011). Since 1991, Cohen has been editor of *Boston Review*. He is on the faculty of Apple University and teaches courses at Stanford's Hasso Plattner Institute of Design (d.school) on using design thinking to develop innovative mobile solutions to problems of poverty and development.

Russell J. Dalton

Russell J. Dalton is a professor of political science at the University of California, Irvine, and was the founding director of the Center for the Study of Democracy at UC Irvine. His recent publications include *The Good Citizen* (2009) and *Democratic Challenges, Democratic Choices* (2004); he is coeditor of *Citizens, Context, and Choice* (2010), *Party Politics in East Asia* (2008), *The Oxford Handbook of Political Behavior* (2007), *Citizens, Democracy, and Markets around the Pacific Rim* (2006), *Democracy Transformed?* (2003), and *Parties without Partisans* (2001). His scholarly interests include comparative political behavior, political parties, social movements, and empirical democratic theory.

Richard Elgar

Richard Elgar is the assistant director of the Thomas S. Foley Institute for Public Policy and Public Service and a doctoral candidate in the Department of Political Science at Washington State University.

Edward A. Feiner

Edward A. Feiner serves as director of the Perkins+Will Design Leadership Forum. The forum, which includes all Perkins+Will design principals, is chartered to ensure the continuity and furtherance of design excellence throughout the firm. Feiner is considered to be among the leading experts in the United States on public buildings design and planning, most notably for the design of courthouses. In 2009, he assumed a leadership position in the Washington, D.C., office as a firm-wide resource. He is best known for his role as chief architect of the U.S. General Services Administration from 1996 until 2005, where he led the agency's nationwide design and construction program, including the development of federal courthouses, office buildings, national laboratories, border stations, and special-use projects.

Theodore L. Glasser

Theodore L. Glasser is a professor of communication at Stanford University, where for 15 years he directed the graduate journalism program. His books include *Normative Theories of the Media: Journalism in Democratic Society*, written with Clifford Christians, Kaarle Nordenstreng, Denis McQuail, and Robert White; *Custodians of Conscience: Investigative Journalism and Public Virtue*, written with James Ettema; *Public Opinion and the Communication of Consent*, edited with Charles Salmon; and *The Idea of Public Journalism*. He has held visiting appointments as a Senior Fulbright Scholar at the Hebrew University of Jerusalem, Israel; as the Wee Kim Wee Professor of Communication Studies at Nanyang Technological University, Singapore; and at the University of Tampere, Finland.

Michael Kazin

Michael Kazin is a professor of history at Georgetown University and coeditor of *Dissent*. He writes about the history of politics and social movements in the United States and is a regular columnist for the *New Republic Online* and a frequent contributor to the *New York Times, Washington Post, Nation, American Prospect*, and other periodicals. His books include *American Dreamers: How the Left Changed a Nation* (to be published in August), *A*

Godly Hero: The Life of William Jennings Bryan, *The Populist Persuasion: An American History*, *Barons of Labor: The San Francisco Building Trades and Union Power in the Progressive Era*, and, with Maurice Isserman, *America Divided: The Civil War of the 1960s*, now in its fourth edition.

Brian Leiter

Brian Leiter is the John P. Wilson Professor of Law and director of the Center for Law, Philosophy, and Human Values at the University of Chicago. He teaches and writes primarily in the areas of moral, political, and legal philosophy, in both Anglophone and continental traditions. His books include *Nietzsche on Morality* (2002) and *Naturalizing Jurisprudence* (2007).

Ann Levey

Ann Levey is an associate professor at the University of Calgary. She has published articles on feminism and on property rights. Other interests include urban philosophy and the philosophy of David Hume. She is currently working on two projects, the role of the family in Hume's political theory, and public space and civility.

Fredrik Logevall

Fredrik Logevall is the John S. Knight Professor of International Studies and professor of history at Cornell, where he serves as director of the Mario Einaudi Center for International Studies. His most recent works are *America's Cold War: The Politics of Insecurity* (with Campbell Craig, Belknap Press/Harvard UP, 2009) and *A People and a Nation: A History of the United States* (9th ed., with Mary Beth Norton et al, Cengage, 2011). His book *Twilight War: The End and the Beginning in Vietnam* is forthcoming from Random House.

Joan Ockman

Joan Ockman is an architectural historian, critic, educator, and editor. From 1994 to 2008 she directed the Temple Hoyne Buell Center for the Study of American Architecture at Columbia University's Graduate School of Architecture, Planning, and Preservation. She is currently teaching at the University of Pennsylvania and has previously held appointments at Cornell, Yale, the Berlage Institute in Rotterdam, the Graduate Center of City University of New York, and the State University of New York at Buffalo. Among the many publications she has edited, her award-winning volume *Architecture Culture 1943–1968*, published in 1993, is currently in its fifth edition. Her other books include *Architourism: Authentic, Escapist, Exotic,*

Spectacular (2005), *Out of Ground Zero: Case Studies in Urban Reinvention* (2002), and *The Pragmatist Imagination: Thinking about Things in the Making* (2001). The American Institute of Architects honored her with an award for collaborative achievement in 2003. She is currently editing a book on the history of architecture education in North America.

Lawrence Pintak

Lawrence Pintak is the founding dean of the Edward R. Murrow College of Communication at Washington State University. A former CBS News Middle East correspondent and veteran of more than 30 years in journalism on four continents, he now writes and lectures on America's relationship with the Muslim world, the role of the media in shaping global perceptions and government policy, and the future of journalism in a digital/globalized world. Pintak's books include *The New Arab Journalist* (I.B. Tauris, 2010), *Reflections in a Bloodshot Lens: America, Islam, and the War of Ideas* (2006), *Seeds of Hate* (2003), and *Beirut Outtakes* (1988). He holds a doctorate in Islamic studies from the University of Wales.

Alan J. Plattus

Alan J. Plattus is a professor of architecture and urbanism at the Yale University School of Architecture, where he teaches courses on architectural history and theory, urban history and design, and directs the school's China Studio. He founded and directs the Yale Urban Design Workshop, a community design center that has undertaken urban design and building projects throughout Connecticut and around the world. Current projects include plans for the cities of West Haven, New London, and Bridgeport, Connecticut; a 13-unit affordable housing project in Bridgeport; a study for the Naugatuck Valley Industrial Heritage Corridor; and the development of a Peace Park along the Jordan River between Israel and Jordan. Research interests include industrial and postindustrial cities in the United States and abroad, urban design history and theory, and sustainable urbanism.

Amanda Porterfield

Amanda Porterfield is the Robert A. Spivey Professor of Religion and professor of history at Florida State University. She is the author of a number of books on American religious history and the history of Christianity and currently serves as the coeditor of the quarterly journal *Church History: Studies in Christianity and Culture*. Her most recent book, *Early American Doubt: Religion, Politics, and Suspicion*, is scheduled for publication in 2012.

Ayad Rahmani

Ayad Rahmani is a professor of architecture at Washington State University, where he teaches courses in design and theory. He is the coauthor of a book on eastern Islamic cities and has a longstanding interest in the cross-disciplinary relationship between architecture and literature. His book on Kafka's architecture is forthcoming with Fordham University Press.

Wade Clark Roof

Wade Clark Roof is the J.F. Rowny Professor of Religion and Society and director of the Walter H. Capps Center for the Study of Ethics, Religion, and Public Life at the University of California, Santa Barbara. He is currently engaged in research on religious pluralism in Southern California.

Witold Rybczynski

Witold Rybczynski is currently the Martin and Margy Meyerson Professor of Urbanism at the University of Pennsylvania. His architectural experience has included designing houses as a registered architect as well as researching low-cost housing, for which he received a 1991 Progressive Architecture Award. In 1993, he was made an honorary fellow of the American Institute of Architects, and he has received honorary doctorates from McGill University and the University of Western Ontario. In 2007, he received the Vincent Scully Prize, the Seaside Prize, and the Institute Collaborative Honors from the AIA. He serves on the U.S. Commission of Fine Arts.

Dietram A. Scheufele

Dietram A. Scheufele holds the John E. Ross Chair in Science Communication at the University of Wisconsin-Madison, and is co-PI of the Center for Nanotechnology in Society at Arizona State University. He has published over 100 peer-refereed articles, book chapters, and monographs dealing with public opinion on emerging technologies and the political effects of mass communication. Scheufele currently cochairs the National Conference of Lawyers and Scientists, a joint committee of the American Association for the Advancement of Science and the American Bar Association, and is a former member of the Nanotechnology Technical Advisory Group of the U.S. President's Council of Advisors on Science and Technology.

Thomas J. Sugrue

Thomas J. Sugrue is the David Boies Professor of History and Sociology at the University of Pennsylvania. Sugrue is the author of *Not Even Past: Barack Obama and the Burden of Race* (Princeton University Press, 2010) and *Sweet Land of Liberty: The Forgotten Struggle for Civil Rights in the North* (Random House, 2008), a main selection of the History Book Club and a finalist for the 2008 Los Angeles Times Book Prize. His first book, *The Origins of the Urban Crisis* (Princeton, 1996), won several awards, including the Bancroft Prize in American History. He is currently writing a history of 20th century America with Glenda Gilmore and working on a history of real estate in the modern United States.

Matthew Avery Sutton

Matthew Avery Sutton is an associate professor of history at Washington State University. His first book, *Aimee Semple McPherson and the Resurrection of Christian America* (Harvard University Press, 2007), won the Thomas J. Wilson Memorial Prize from Harvard University Press, awarded annually to the best book in any discipline by a first-time author. He is currently working on a new book, *American Evangelicals and the Politics of Apocalypse* (Harvard University Press, forthcoming 2012), which examines the relationships among American evangelicalism, apocalyptic thought, and political activism in times of national crisis and war; and a textbook, *Jerry Falwell and the Origins of the Religious Right*, which will be part of the popular Bedford Series in History and Culture (Bedford/St. Martin's, forthcoming 2012). He has received research fellowships from the National Endowment for the Humanities and the Woodrow Wilson Fellowship Foundation.